everyday Comprehension

Intervention Activities

Table of Contents

Using Everyday Comprehension Intervention Activities

Reading with full text comprehension is the ultimate goal of all reading instruction. Students who read the words but don't comprehend them aren't really reading at all. Research has shown that explicit comprehension strategy instruction helps students understand and remember what they read, which allows them to communicate what they've learned with others and perform better in testing situations.

Although some students master comprehension strategies easily during regular classroom instruction, many others need additional re-teaching opportunities to master these essential strategies. The Everyday Intervention Activities series provides easy-to-use, five-day intervention units for Grades K–5. These units are structured around a research-based Model-Guide-Practice-Apply approach. You can use these activities in a variety of intervention models, including Response to Intervention (RTI).

Getting Started

In just five simple steps, Everyday Comprehension Intervention Activities provides everything you need to identify students' comprehension needs and to provide targeted, research-based intervention.

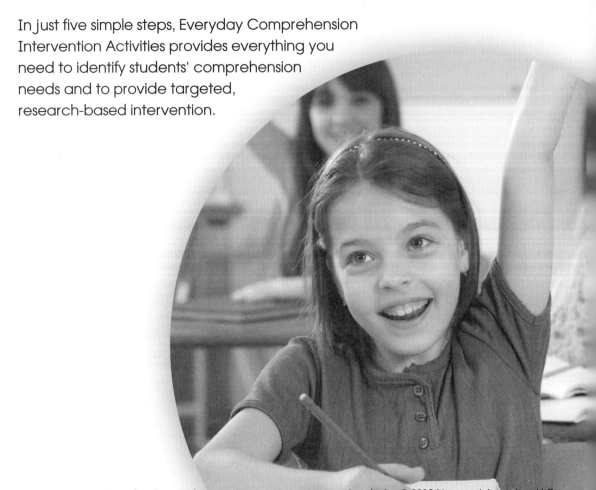

1. PRE-ASSESS to identify students' comprehension needs.

Use the pre-assessment to identify the strategies your students need to master.

2. MODEL the strategy.

Every five-day unit targets a specific strategy. On Day 1, use the teacher prompts and reproducible activity to introduce and model the strategy.

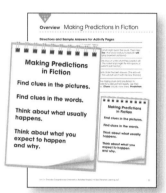

3. GUIDE PRACTICE and APPLY.

Use the reproducible practice activities for Days 2, 3, and 4 to build students' understanding of, and proficiency with, the strategy.

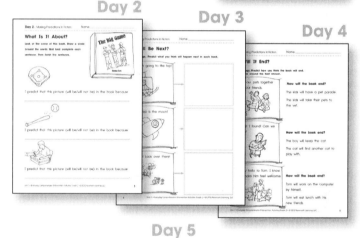

4. MONITOR progress.

Administer the Day 5 reproducible assessment to monitor each student's progress and to make instructional decisions.

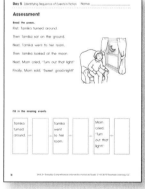

5. POST-ASSESS to document student progress.

Use the post-assessment to measure students' progress as a result of your interventions.

Standards-Based Comprehension Strategies in Everyday Intervention Activities

The comprehension strategies found in the Everyday Intervention Activities series are introduced developmentally and spiral from one grade to the next based on curriculum standards across a variety of states. The chart below shows the comprehension strategies addressed at each grade level in this series.

Comprehension Strategy	Strategy Definition	K	1	2	3	4	5
Make Predictions	Determine what might happen next in a story or nonfiction piece. Predictions are based on information presented in the text.	✔	✔	✔	✔	✔	✔
Identify Sequence of Events	Determine the order of events for topics such as history, science, or biography. Determine the steps to make or do something.	✔	✔	✔	✔	✔	✔
Analyze Story Elements	Analyze the setting and plot (problem/solution) in a fiction text.	✔	✔	✔	✔	✔	✔
Analyze Character	Analyze story characters based on information and on clues and evidence in the text, including description, actions, dialogue, feelings, and traits.	✔	✔	✔	✔	✔	✔
Identify Main Idea and Supporting Details	Determine what the paragraph, page, or chapter is mostly about. Sometimes the main idea is stated and sometimes it is implied. Students must choose details that support the main idea, not "just any detail."	✔	✔	✔	✔	✔	✔
Summarize	Take key ideas from the text and put them together to create a shorter version of the original text. Summaries should have few, if any, details.	✔	✔	✔	✔	✔	✔
Compare and Contrast	Find ways that two things are alike and different.	✔	✔	✔	✔	✔	✔
Identify Cause and Effect	Find things that happened (effect) and why they happened (cause). Text may contain multiple causes and effects.	✔	✔	✔	✔	✔	✔
Make Inferences	Determine what the author is suggesting without directly stating it. Inferences are usually made during reading and are made from one or two pieces of information from the text. Students' inferences will vary but must be made from the evidence in the text and background knowledge.	✔	✔	✔	✔	✔	✔
Draw Conclusions	Determine what the author is suggesting without directly stating it. Conclusions are made during and after reading, and are made from multiple (3+) pieces of information from the text. Students' conclusions will vary but must be drawn from the evidence in the text and background knowledge.		✔	✔	✔	✔	✔
Evaluate Author's Purpose	Determine why the author wrote the passage or used certain information. A book can have more than one purpose. Purposes include to entertain, to inform, and to persuade.			✔	✔	✔	✔
Analyze Text Structure and Organization	Determine the text structure to better understand what the author is saying and to use as research when text must be analyzed.			✔	✔	✔	✔
Use Text Features to Locate Information	Use text features (bullets, captions, glossary, index, sidebars) to enhance meaning.			✔	✔	✔	✔
Use Graphic Features to Interpret Information	Use clues from graphic features (charts, maps, graphs) to determine what is not stated in the text or to enhance meaning.			✔	✔	✔	✔
Distinguish and Evaluate Facts and Opinions	Recognize objective statements of fact and subjective opinions within a nonfiction text.					✔	✔
Make Judgments	Use facts from the text and prior knowledge and beliefs to make and confirm opinions about the characters or situations.					✔	✔

Using Everyday Intervention for RTI

According to the National Center on Response to Intervention, RTI "integrates assessment and intervention within a multi-level prevention system to maximize student achievement and to reduce behavior problems." This model of instruction and assessment allows schools to identify at-risk students, monitor their progress, provide research-proven interventions, and "adjust the intensity and nature of those interventions depending on a student's responsiveness."

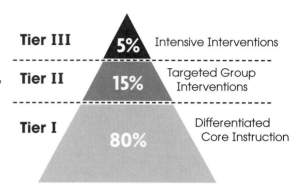

RTI models vary from district to district, but the most prevalent model is a three-tiered approach to instruction and assessment.

The Three Tiers of RTI	Using Everyday Intervention Activities
Tier I: Differentiated Core Instruction • Designed for all students • Preventive, proactive, standards-aligned instruction • Whole- and small-group differentiated instruction • Ninety-minute, daily core reading instruction in the five essential skill areas: phonics, phonemic awareness, comprehension, vocabulary, fluency	• Use whole-group comprehension mini-lessons to introduce and guide practice with comprehension strategies that all students need to learn. • Use any or all of the units in the order that supports your core instructional program.
Tier II: Targeted Group Interventions • For at-risk students • Provide thirty minutes of daily instruction beyond the ninety-minute Tier I core reading instruction • Instruction is conducted in small groups of three to five students with similar needs	• Select units based on your students' areas of need (the pre-assessment can help you identify these). • Use the units as week-long, small-group mini-lessons.
Tier III: Intensive Interventions • For high-risk students experiencing considerable difficulty in reading • Provide up to sixty minutes of additional intensive intervention each day in addition to the ninety-minute Tier I core reading instruction • More intense and explicit instruction • Instruction conducted individually or with smaller groups of one to three students with similar needs	• Select units based on your students' areas of need. • Use the units as one component of an intensive comprehension intervention program.

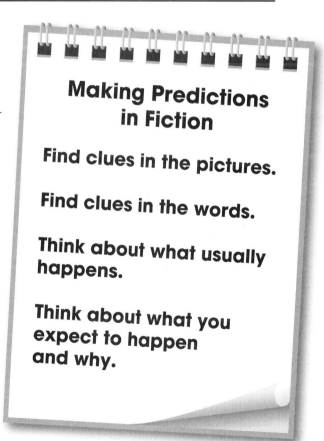

Overview Making Predictions in Fiction

Directions and Sample Answers for Activity Pages

Day 1	See "Provide a Real-World Example" below.
Day 2	Discuss the book cover. Ask students to predict what might be in the book. Then help students complete the correct sentences. (**will be**—the book is about baseball; **will be**—a ball is part of baseball; **will not be**—you play baseball outdoors)
Day 3	Read and discuss each page. Then help students draw or write what they predict will happen next. (The bear might ski down the hill. The rocket ship might fly into space or land on the moon. The bees might fly to the flowers to eat nectar.)
Day 4	Read and discuss each page. Then help students circle the best answer. (The kids will have a pet parade. The boy will keep the cat. Tom will eat lunch with his new friends.)
Day 5	Read the story together. Ask students to fill in the missing clues and prediction in the chart. Afterward, meet individually with students to discuss their results. Use their responses to plan further instruction and review. (**Clues:** clouds, new dress. **Prediction:** Kimora will take an umbrella.)

Provide a Real-World Example

◆ Hand out the Day 1 activity page.

◆ **Say:** *I have a friend who loves horses. She talks about horses and reads about horses. I can usually predict— or make a good guess about—what my friend will do on the weekend. What do you predict my friend will do this weekend?*

◆ Allow time for students to respond. Then ask them to look at the pictures and color the picture that matches their prediction.

◆ **Say:** *I have another friend who likes to work at his computer. He designs Web pages and does research on the Internet. What do you predict my friend will do this weekend? Color the picture that matches your prediction.*

◆ Explain that students can also predict, or make a good guess, when they read stories. Write the following on chart paper:

Making Predictions in Fiction

Find clues in the pictures.

Find clues in the words.

Think about what usually happens.

Think about what you expect to happen and why.

What Will They Do?

Listen to the activity. Then color the picture that shows your prediction.

Listen to the activity. Then color the picture that shows your prediction.

Unit 1 • Everyday Comprehension Intervention Activities Grade 2 • © 2010 Newmark Learning, LLC

What Is It About?

Look at the cover of this book. Draw a circle around the words that best complete each sentence. Then finish the sentences.

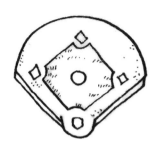

I predict that this picture (will be/will not be) in the book because

_____.

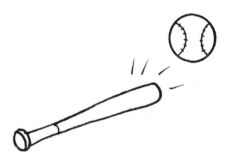

I predict that this picture (will be/will not be) in the book because

_____.

I predict that this picture (will be/will not be) in the book because

_____.

Name _____

What Will Be Next?

Read each page. Predict what you think will happen next in each book.

     Unit 1 • Everyday Comprehension Intervention Activities Grade 2 • © 2010 Newmark Learning, LLC

Name _____

How Will It End?

Read the page. Predict how you think the book will end.

Draw a circle around the best answer.

Let's get our pets together to show our friends.

How will the book end?

The kids will have a pet parade.

The kids will take their pets to the vet.

Look what I found! Can we feed her?

How will the book end?

The boy will keep the cat.

The cat will find another cat to play with.

Please say hello to Tom. I know you will make him feel welcome.

How will the book end?

Tom will work on the computer by himself.

Tom will eat lunch with his new friends.

Assessment

Read the passage. Write the clues. Then write what you predict Kimora will do.

"Be sure to take an umbrella, Kimora," Mom called. "I see rain clouds."

Kimora sighed. "I hate carrying an umbrella. Besides, the sun was shining earlier."

"It's up to you," Mom replied. "But remember—you're wearing your new dress."

Clues	**Prediction**

Overview Making Predictions in Nonfiction

Directions and Sample Answers for Activity Pages

Day 1	See "Provide a Real-World Example" below.
Day 2	Discuss the book cover. Ask students to predict what might be in the book. Then help students complete the correct sentences. (**will be**—the book is about a map; **will not be**—a house doesn't have a science lab; **will be**—the book is about the house the girl's family lives in)
Day 3	Read and discuss each page. Then help students draw or write what they predict will happen next. (The boy and his classmates might use the pencils to write or draw. The girl might water the plants with the hose. The boy might check out some books.)
Day 4	Read and discuss each page. Then help students circle the best answers. (ask readers to think of ways to help animals; show readers how to draw a cone; ask readers how people might communicate in the future)
Day 5	Read the ad together. Ask students to predict what will happen when people read the ad. Afterward, meet individually with students to discuss their results. Use their responses to plan further instruction and review. (**Evidence:** cute, free, free bag of cat food. **Prediction:** The writer will give away all the kittens.)

Provide a Real-World Example

◆ Hand out the Day 1 activity page.

◆ **Ask:** *What day is tomorrow? What do you usually do at 8:00 in the morning on that day? What do you predict you will do at 8:00 tomorrow morning?*

◆ Allow time for students to draw or write their predictions beside the top clock.

◆ Repeat the process with the clock that says 12:00 (noon) and the clock that says 5:00 (in the afternoon).

◆ Invite students to share their predictions with a partner. Then explain that they can also make predictions when they read. Write the following on chart paper:

Making Predictions in Nonfiction

Find evidence in the pictures.

Find evidence in the words.

Think about what usually happens.

Think about what you expect to happen and why.

Tomorrow

Look at each clock. Then make predictions of what you will do tomorrow at that time.

A Map of My House

Look at the cover of this book.
Draw a circle around the words that best
complete the sentence. Then finish the sentence.

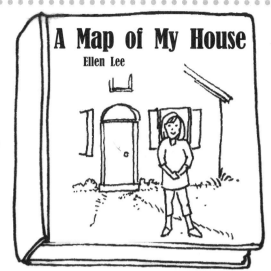

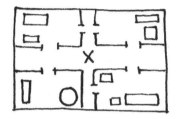

I predict that this picture (will be/will not be) in the
book because _____
_____ .

I predict that this picture (will be/will not be) in the
book because _____
_____ .

I predict that this picture (will be/will not be) in the
book because _____
_____ .

What's Next?

Read the page. Predict what you think will happen next in the book.

People use pencils at school.

People care for plants.

People get books at the library.

The End

Read the page. Predict how you think the book will end.
Draw a circle around the best answer.

Animals need many things.
People can help animals.

The author will . . .

• ask readers to think of ways
  to help animals

• tell why dogs make the best pets

You can see cones all
around. Some houses have
a cone on top.

The author will . . .

• tell about some other types
  of houses

• show readers how to draw
  a cone

Do you send e-mails? Do
you talk on the phone? You
can communicate!

The author will . . .

• tell readers they should send
  more e-mails

• ask readers how people might
  communicate in the future

Assessment

Read the ad. Write the clues.

Then predict what you think will happen.

Free!

Fluffy kittens.

Very cute. Free bag of
cat food with each kitten.

Evidence	**Prediction**

          Unit 2 • Everyday Comprehension Intervention Activities Grade 2 • © 2010 Newmark Learning, LLC

Overview Identifying Sequence of Events in Fiction

Directions and Sample Answers for Activity Pages

Day 1	See "Provide a Real-World Example" below.
Day 2	Discuss the pictures. Then help students cut out the pictures, put them in the correct order, and glue them onto another sheet of paper. (dogs see bone, dogs stand over bone, dogs growl over bone, dogs decide to share the bone and walk away)
Day 3	Read and discuss the story. Then help students draw lines to show the correct order. (He thought about Gramma. He got a pencil and paper. He sat at the table. He wrote a letter.)
Day 4	Read and discuss the story. Then help students number the pictures in the correct order. (3, 1, 4, 2)
Day 5	Read the poem together. Ask students to fill in the missing steps in the chart. Afterward, meet individually with students to discuss their results. Use their responses to plan further instruction and review. (Tamika sat on the ground. Tamika looked at the moon. Mom said, "Sweet good-night!")

Provide a Real-World Example

◆ Hand out the Day 1 activity page.

◆ **Say:** *Last weekend, my friend went to the library. First, she walked in the door. Then she took a book from the shelf. Next, she looked through the book. Finally, she took the book to the check-out desk. My friend did all these things in a certain order, or sequence. First she did one thing, then another, another, and another.*

◆ Ask students to look at the pictures and write the number 1 to show what happened first on the trip to the library. Repeat with the other three events. Then invite them to share other things people do in a certain order.

◆ Explain that students can also find a sequence of events when they read stories. Write the following on chart paper:

Identifying Sequence of Events in Fiction

Find clues in the pictures.

Find words that tell about order, such as *first, next, then*, and *after that*.

Think about the order in which things usually happen.

The Library

Listen. Next, look at the pictures. Then number the pictures to show the correct order.

One Bone

Look at the pictures of two dogs and one bone.
Cut out the pictures. Put them in the correct order.
Then glue them onto another sheet of paper.

Letter to Gramma

Read the story.

Jim was sad. He thought about his grandmother.

Then he got paper and a pencil. Next, he sat at the table.

He wrote a letter. "Dear Gramma," he wrote. "I miss you."

Draw lines to answer the questions.

What did Jim do first?

He wrote a letter.

Then what did Jim do?

He thought about Gramma.

What did Jim do next?

He sat at the table.

What did Jim do after that?

He got a pencil and paper.

Pet Party

Read the story.

Mia decided to have a party for her pets.

First, she put out dishes. Then she put out snacks. Next, she found her pets. Her pets did not want a party, though. They ran away!

Number the pictures to show the correct order.

Assessment

Read the poem.

First, Tamika turned around.

Then Tamika sat on the ground.

Next, Tamika went to her room.

Then Tamika looked at the moon.

Next, Mom cried, "Turn out that light!"

Finally, Mom said, "Sweet good-night!"

Fill in the missing events

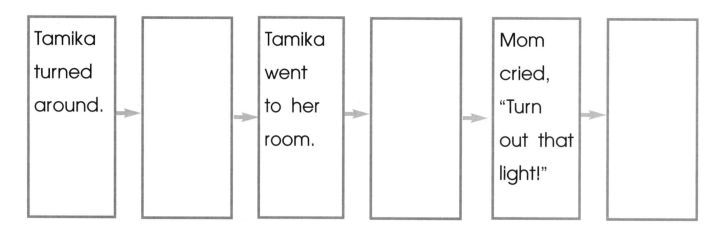

| Tamika turned around. | | Tamika went to her room. | | Mom cried, "Turn out that light!" | |

Overview Identifying Sequence of Events in Nonfiction

Directions and Sample Answers for Activity Pages

Day 1	See "Provide a Real-World Example" below.
Day 2	Read the passage together. Then help students cut out the pictures, put them in the correct order, and glue them onto another sheet of paper. (rolling large snowball, stacking snowballs, rolling small snowball, putting face on)
Day 3	Discuss the pictures. Then help students number the sentences in the correct order. (3, 2, 1, 4)
Day 4	Read and discuss the passage. Then help students number the pictures in the correct order. (3, 1, 4, 2)
Day 5	Read the report together. Ask students to fill in the missing events on the graphic organizer. Afterward, meet individually with students to discuss their results. Use their responses to plan further instruction and review. (We went to the Tiger Forest. We watched the monkeys play. We saw the snakes.)

Provide a Real-World Example

◆ Hand out the Day 1 activity page.

◆ **Say:** *This morning, I saw a man crossing the street. First, the man stopped at the corner. Next, he looked both ways. Finally, he walked across the street. Doing things in a certain order is called a sequence of events.*

◆ Ask students to mark what the man did first with the number **1**. Ask them to mark the picture that shows what happened next with the number **2**. Ask them to write the number **3** under the picture that shows what the man did last.

◆ **Say:** *Now look at the next row of pictures. This time, a child needs to cross the street to go to school. Put a number **1** on the picture that shows what the child should do first. Write a number **2** on the picture that shows what the child should do next. Write a **3** on the picture that shows what the child should do last.*

◆ Explain that students can also find sequence of events when they read. Write the following on chart paper:

Identifying Sequence of Events in Nonfiction

Find evidence in the pictures.

Find words that tell about order, such as *first, then, next, finally,* and *last.*

Think about the order in which things usually happen.

Crossing the Street

Listen. Then number the boxes to show the correct order.

Listen. Then number the boxes to show the correct order.

Making a Snowman

Read the passage.

You can make a snowman. First, roll two big snowballs. Then put one snowball on top of the other. Next, roll a small snowball for the head. Finally, put a face on the snowman.

Cut out the pictures. Put them in the correct order. Then glue them onto another sheet of paper.

Dog Wash

Sometimes a dog needs a bath. Look at the pictures.

Number the sentences in the correct order.

__ Wash the dog.

__ Put the dog in the tub.

__ Fill a tub with water.

__ Rinse the dog.

Packing Up

Read the passage.

Do you know how to pack a picnic basket?
Dishes are heavy, so put them in first.
Then put in the spoons and forks.
Next, put in the sandwiches. Put the fruit
in last.

Number the pictures in the correct order.

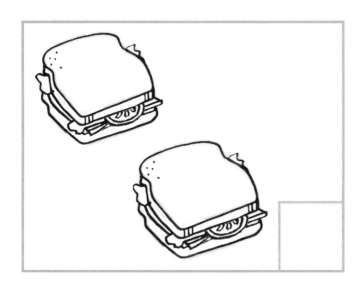

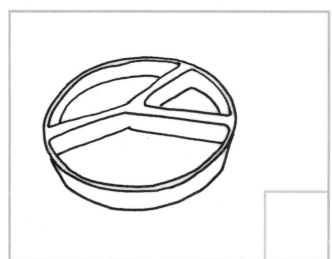

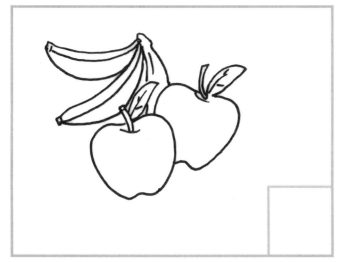

Assessment

Read the report about a class field trip.

This week we took a trip to the zoo. First, we got our tickets. Next, we went to the Tiger Forest. We watched the tigers for a long time. Then we ate lunch near the rain forest.

After lunch, we watched the monkeys play. The last animals we saw were the snakes. Finally, we left the zoo. We were tired and happy.

Fill in the missing events.

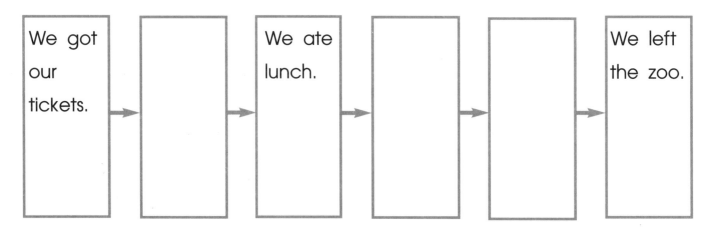

| We got our tickets. | | We ate lunch. | | | We left the zoo. |

Overview Analyzing Story Elements: Setting

Directions and Sample Answers for Activity Pages

Day 1	See "Provide a Real-World Example" below.
Day 2	Discuss each picture. Then help students identify and color the pictures that show setting. (street, kitchen, ball field, forest, bird cage)
Day 3	Read and discuss each phrase. Help students identify and circle the phrases that tell about settings. Then help students write another phrase about a setting. (a dark night, my bedroom, the gym, the zoo, early morning, a flower shop)
Day 4	Read and discuss each passage. Then help students underline the setting clues and write when and where each story takes place. (**Clues:** long ago, castle, large. **Setting:** long ago in a large castle. **Clues:** dirty, cabin, moonlight, snow. **Setting:** a snowy night in a dirty cabin.)
Day 5	Read the passage together. Ask students to record the setting clues and setting on their graphic organizers. Afterward, meet individually with students to discuss their results. Use their responses to plan further instruction and review. (**Clues:** Sunie, door, bed, curtains, stuffed animals, books, desk. **Setting:** daytime in Sunie's bedroom.)

Provide a Real-World Example

◆ Hand out the Day 1 activity page.

◆ **Say:** *Today we will talk about setting. A setting is when and where something takes place. We are in a setting right now. I see sunlight through the window. The sunlight is a clue. I see clues in the room, too. I see desks and chairs. I see books and computers. I see students. These clues tell me that our setting is daytime in a classroom.*

◆ Invite students to look at the pictures and describe the settings they see. With a partner, invite them to imagine a story that could happen in one of these settings.

◆ **Ask:** *What other settings can you think of? Remember that the place can be real or imaginary. The time can be now, in the past, or in the future.*

◆ Explain that students can also analyze settings when they read stories. Write the following on chart paper:

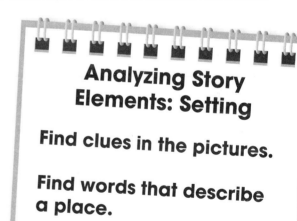

Analyzing Story Elements: Setting

Find clues in the pictures.

Find words that describe a place.

Find words that tell about a time.

Think about when and where an event could happen.

What Could Happen Here?

Look at the pictures. Talk about each setting. Then imagine a story in one of the following settings.

Name _____

Places

Look at the pictures. Color the pictures that show a setting.

When and Where

Read each phrase. Draw a circle around each phrase that tells about a setting.

a dark night

the team

my best friend

the gym

my bedroom

time to go

the zoo

a sad boy

early morning

a flower shop

Write another phrase that tells about a setting.

_____

Setting Clues

**Read each passage. Draw a line under the setting clues.
Then write when and where the story takes place.**

Long ago, a queen lived in a castle with many large rooms. The queen had two children, a boy and a girl. The children ran from room to room when they played.

This story takes place _____ in a _____ .

Tony and Jeff sat close together on the dirty cabin floor. No moonlight shone through the window. They could hear the wind howl as snow piled against the door.

"I'm scared!" said Jeff.

This story takes place _____ in a _____ .

Assessment

Read the passage.

Sunie closed the door and fell on her soft bed. The sun poured past the flowered curtains. Stuffed animals sat on the shelves. Her favorite books were piled on her desk.

Write the clues. Then name the setting.

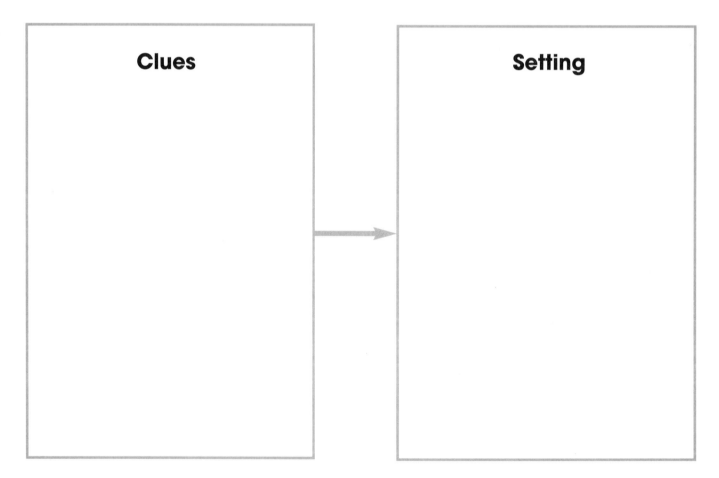

Clues	Setting

Overview Analyzing Story Elements: Plot

Directions and Sample Answers for Activity Pages

Day 1	See "Provide a Real-World Example" below.
Day 2	Discuss the pictures. Then help students identify and color the picture that shows the beginning of each plot. (the sad bird in the cage; the space creature saying "I'm hungry!")
Day 3	Discuss the pictures. Then help students draw or write what might happen in the middle of each plot. (Responses will vary.)
Day 4	Read the beginning and middle of the story together. Discuss. Then help students select and circle the best ending. (Grandpa loved Mira's dance.)
Day 5	Read the story together. Ask students to write what happened at the beginning, middle, and end of the story. Afterward, meet individually with students to discuss their results. Use their responses to plan further instruction and review. (**Beginning:** Reeba lost her homework. **Middle:** She looked for it. **End:** She found it. Her baby brother had it!)

Provide a Real-World Example

◆ Hand out the Day 1 activity page.

◆ **Say:** *Imagine a group of kids getting ready for a baseball game. Suddenly, it begins to rain. What will they do? They decide to wait under the picnic shelter. Soon, the sun comes out, and the game begins.*

◆ Ask students to Think/Pair/Share other things the kids could have done. Then **say:** *These events are like the plot of a story. The beginning of the story tells a problem. The middle of the story tells what the characters do. The end of the story tells the solution to the problem.*

◆ Write the words **beginning**, **middle**, and **end** on the board. Ask students to look at the top row of pictures and write the correct word under each picture. Then discuss the pictures on the bottom row and help students label the story parts.

◆ Explain that students can also analyze plots when they read stories. Write the following on chart paper:

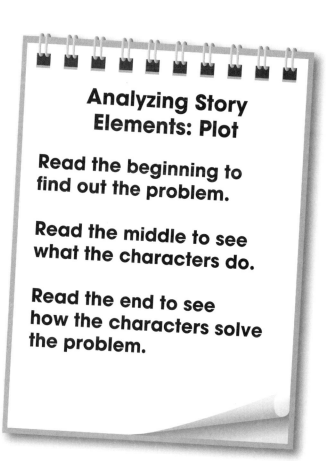

Analyzing Story Elements: Plot

Read the beginning to find out the problem.

Read the middle to see what the characters do.

Read the end to see how the characters solve the problem.

Stories

Look at each row of pictures. Then label each picture *beginning*, *middle*, or *end* to show the plot.

_____   _____   _____

_____   _____   _____

Story Starters

Look at the pictures. Color the picture that shows the beginning of each plot.

Name _____

In the Middle

Look at the pictures. Draw or write what might happen in the middle of each plot.

Unit 6 • Everyday Comprehension Intervention Activities Grade 2 • © 2010 Newmark Learning, LLC

The Show

**Read the beginning and middle of the plot.
Then draw a circle around the best ending.**

Beginning

"Tonight is the show!" said Mira.

"I have to dance in front of the whole school!

I'm scared!"

Middle

"What would make you feel better?" asked Mom.

"Maybe I could dance for Grandpa," said Mira.

"If he likes it, I'll be fine."

"Let's get in the car," said Mom.

End

Grandpa wasn't home.

"I'm sorry, Mira," said Mom.

"Maybe Grandpa will come to the show."

Grandpa loved Mira's dance!

"Thanks, Grandpa," Mira said.

"Now I'm not scared anymore."

"You can dance some other time," said Grandpa.

"Let's watch a movie."

"OK!" said Mira.

Assessment

Read the story.

Reeba could not find her homework.

It was time for the bus!

She looked in her room.

She looked under the sofa.

She looked in the kitchen.

In walked Reeba's baby brother.

He had a paper in his hand.

"Look," he said with a smile.

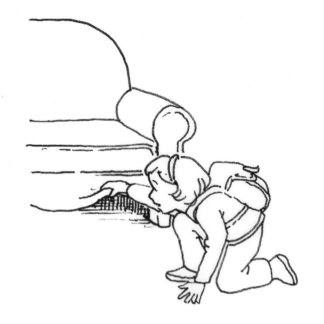

Write what happened at the beginning, middle, and end of the story.

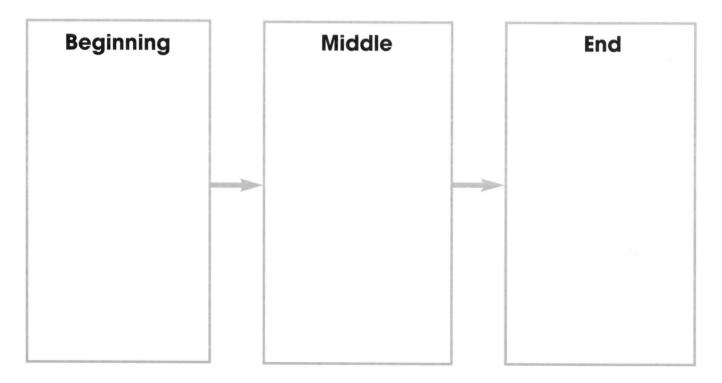

Beginning	**Middle**	**End**

Overview Analyzing Character: Traits

Directions and Sample Answers for Activity Pages

Day 1	See "Provide a Real-World Example" below.
Day 2	Ask each student to draw a picture of someone he or she knows well. Then have them complete the sentences to describe the person's traits. Remind them that the "because" part of the sentence should contain a clue about the trait. (**Example:** My sister is generous because she always shares things with her friends.)
Day 3	Read and discuss the story. Then ask students to circle Tia's traits and write a clue for one of the traits. (**Traits:** smart, bossy, fair. **Clue for "smart":** made up a new game.)
Day 4	Read about Lady and Shadow together. Discuss. Then ask students to circle the best answer to each question and explain their answers. (**Friendly:** Lady—barks to say "hello," loves people. **Helpful:** Shadow—helps Mr. Parks. **Athletic:** Lady—always ready to play ball; flies across the grass. **Calm:** Shadow—quiet, likes to nap.)
Day 5	Read the passage together. Ask students to write clues about Jazzy and name one of her traits on their graphic organizers. Afterward, meet individually with students to discuss their results. Use their responses to plan further instruction and review. (**Clues:** sat next to new girl at lunch; talked the whole time; excited about new friend. **Trait:** friendly.)

Provide a Real-World Example

◆ Hand out the Day 1 activity page.

◆ **Say:** *You are different from your family members and friends. Your family members and friends are different from one another. That is because every person has certain traits, or special features. Being kind is a trait. So is being bossy. Traits show up in the things we think, do, and say.*

◆ Together, read and discuss each trait on the page. Then invite students to put a check mark in front of the traits that describe themselves.

◆ **Say:** *Think of someone in your family or one of your friends. Put a check mark in front of the traits that tell about the other person. Do you share some of the same traits?*

◆ Explain that students can also analyze character traits when they read stories. Write the following on chart paper:

Analyzing Character: Traits

Find clues in the pictures.

Find clues in the words.

Think about what the character thinks, says, and does.

Think of words that describe the character.

All About You

Read and discuss each trait. Then put a check mark next to the traits that describe you and your family member or friend.

Traits

Me	**My Family Member or Friend**
____ kind	____ kind
____ bossy	____ bossy
____ patient	____ patient
____ cheerful	____ cheerful
____ friendly	____ friendly
____ clever	____ clever
____ quiet	____ quiet
____ fair	____ fair

Someone You Know

**Draw a picture of someone you know well.
Then write three sentences about the person's traits.**

```
┌──────────────────────────────────────────────────────────┐
│                                                            │
│                                                            │
│                                                            │
│                                                            │
│                                                            │
│                                                            │
│                                                            │
│                                                            │
│                                                            │
│                                                            │
│                                                            │
│                                                            │
└──────────────────────────────────────────────────────────┘
```

_____ is _____ because _____.

_____ is _____ because _____.

_____ is _____ because _____.

Tia

Read the story.

"We're playing a new game today," said Tia. "I made it up!"

"You always get to pick!" said Martin.

"True," said Tia. "And I always pick fun ones!"

Martin nodded. "Today I want to do it, though."

"Okay!" said Tia. "I can't wait to see which one you pick!"

Draw a circle around Tia's traits.

smart   shy   bossy

patient   selfish   fair

Write a clue for one of Tia's traits.

Trait:_____

Clue:_____

Lady and Shadow

Read about Lady and Shadow.

Two dogs live on our street.

Lady barks to say "hello." She loves
people. She is always ready to play ball.
She flies across the grass to catch the ball.

Shadow is a quiet dog. He helps his owner.
Mr. Parks does not see well. Shadow likes to
nap when he is not with Mr. Parks.

Circle the best answer. Then tell how you know.

Which dog would you say is friendly?   Lady   Shadow

Why? _____

Which dog would you say is helpful?   Lady   Shadow

Why? _____

Which dog would you say is athletic?   Lady   Shadow

Why? _____

Which dog would you say is calm?   Lady   Shadow

Why? _____

Assessment

Read the passage.

Dear Diary,

I made a new friend today!

Her name is Cass. She just moved here.
She looked scared, so I sat next to her
at lunch. We talked the whole time!

We both like to swim. And she loves dogs just like I do.

I am so excited!

    Your friend,

    Jazzy

Write clues about Jazzy. Then name one of her traits.

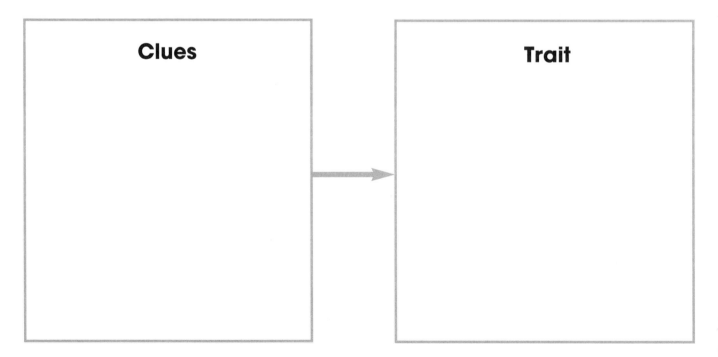

Clues

Trait

Overview Analyzing Character: Feelings

Directions and Sample Answers for Activity Pages

Day 1	See "Provide a Real-World Example" below.
Day 2	Discuss each picture. Then help students complete the sentence to describe how the child feels. (won race/excited or proud; hugging family/happy; seeing large dog/scared)
Day 3	Read and discuss the story. Then help students answer the questions about Sean. (**At first:** puzzled/Sean thought and thought. **After Grandma opened the box:** happy/Grandma said she would smile all day long.)
Day 4	Read and discuss the story. Then help students complete the sentences and write a clue for each feeling. (**Zahir:** scared/What if I forget my lines? **Dad:** proud/That's my son up there!)
Day 5	Read the passage together. Ask students to write clues about Tammy and tell how she feels on their graphic organizers. Afterward, meet individually with students to discuss their results. Use their responses to plan further instruction and review. (**Clues:** loves to write; would write all the time if she could; Ms. Picco likes her stories; friends like her stories; really wants to win the contest. **Feelings:** excited, confident.)

Provide a Real-World Example

◆ Hand out the Day 1 activity page.

◆ **Say:** *We all have different feelings at different times. I remember the first day I was a teacher. I had many different feelings that day! I was excited and happy, but I was nervous, too.*

◆ Together, read and discuss each feeling on the page. Then ask students to think about a time they started going to a new school or started a new school year. Invite them to put a check mark in front of the feelings they had that day.

◆ **Ask:** *What about your classmates? How do you think they felt that day? Put a check mark in front of the feelings they had. Did you share some of the same feelings?*

◆ Explain that students can also find a character's feelings when they read stories. Write the following on chart paper:

Analyzing Character: Feelings

Find clues in the pictures.

Find clues in the words.

Think about what the character thinks, says, and does.

Think of words that describe how the character feels.

The First Day

Read and discuss each feeling. Then put a check mark next to the feelings you and your classmates had on the first day of school.

Feelings

Me	**My Classmates**
_____ eager	_____ eager
_____ calm	_____ calm
_____ worried	_____ worried
_____ excited	_____ excited
_____ lonely	_____ lonely
_____ brave	_____ brave
_____ happy	_____ happy

Name _____

How Do They Feel?

Look at each picture. Then complete the sentence.

This child feels_____

because _____

_____.

This child feels_____

because _____

_____.

This child feels_____

because _____

_____.

Sean and Grandma

Read the story.

"I want to make something for Grandma," said Sean.

"What do you think she would like?" asked Mom.

Sean thought and thought. Then he drew a picture of himself. He put it inside a small box and took it to Grandma.

"Thank you!" said Grandma. "This will make me smile all day long!"

Draw a circle around the best answers. Then answer the questions.

How did Sean feel at first?

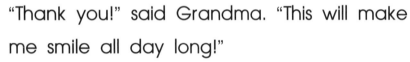

               puzzled   sad

How do you know? _____

How do you think Sean felt after Grandma opened the box?

               brave   happy

Why? _____

The Class Play

Read the story.

Zahir stood on the stage.

Soon it would be his turn to speak.

"Oh no," he thought. "What if I forget my lines?"

Dad sat in the front row.

He smiled and winked at Zahir.

"That's my son up there!" he thought to himself.

Complete the sentences. Then write a clue to tell how you know.

I think Zahir feels _____.

Clue: _____

I think Dad feels _____.

Clue: _____

Name _____

Assessment

Read the passage.

Dear Diary,

We're having a writing contest at school. The best story will win a prize!

A writing contest! I LOVE to write. I would write all the time if I could. Ms. Picco has told me my stories are good. My friends even like them. I just HAVE TO WIN the contest!

Tammy

Write clues about Tammy. Then tell how she feels.

Clues	Feelings

Unit 8 • Everyday Comprehension Intervention Activities Grade 2 • © 2010 Newmark Learning, LLC

Overview Identifying Stated Main Idea

Directions and Sample Answers for Activity Pages

Day 1	See "Provide a Real-World Example" below.
Day 2	Read and discuss the passage. Then help students draw a line under the stated main idea in each paragraph. (Many animals live inside shells. A shell keeps a turtle safe. The shell protects the clam.)
Day 3	Read and discuss the passage. Help students locate and color the stated main idea and the sentence that doesn't belong. Then ask them to color a place on the map they would like to visit. (**1:** A map shows where places are. **2:** Many people like to go to the zoo. **3:** Responses will vary.)
Day 4	Read and discuss the passage. Then help students answer the questions. (**1:** Michelle Kwan. **2:** Michelle Kwan is one of the best skaters of all time. **3:** Responses will vary.)
Day 5	Read the passage together. Ask students to read the supporting details in the second box on the graphic organizer. Then ask them to look back at the passage, find the stated main idea, and write it in the first box. Afterward, meet individually with students to discuss their results. Use their responses to plan further instruction and review. (**Stated main idea:** We can eat some plants.)

Provide a Real-World Example

◆ Hand out the Day 1 activity page.

◆ **Say:** *I saw a film the other day. It was about a farmer's market. I saw many kinds of homegrown fruits and vegetables. I saw homemade cakes, pies, and cookies, too. The woman in the film stated that a farmer's market is a good place to buy food.*

◆ Ask students to draw several things people can buy at a farmer's market. Then help them complete the main idea that the woman in the film stated about a farmer's market.

◆ Explain that they can also find stated main ideas when they read. Write the following on chart paper:

Identifying Stated Main Idea

See what the passage is about.

Find details about the topic.

Find the sentence that tells about the details.

Find the sentence that tells the most important idea.

Name _____

The Farmer's Market

Listen. Draw several things you can buy at a farmer's market.

Then write the stated main idea below.

Stated Main Idea:

A farmer's market is a _____ place to buy _____.

Animal Shells

Read the passage. Draw a line under the stated main idea in each paragraph.

Where does a snail live?

Where does a crab live?

Inside a shell!

Many animals live inside shells.

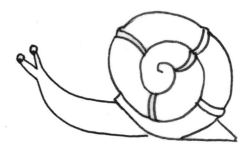

A turtle lives in a shell.

A shell keeps a turtle safe.

The turtle hides inside the shell when danger is near.

A clam lives in a shell.

The clam closes its shell when danger is near.

The shell protects the clam.

Maps

Read the passage.

A map shows where places are.

Some maps have roads and cities.

Some maps have mountains
and lakes.

Some maps even have parks
and zoos.

Many people like to go to the zoo.

You can use a map to find places.

1. **Find the stated main idea. Color it red.**

2. **Find a sentence that does not
belong. Color it blue.**

3. **Find a place on one of these maps
you would like to visit. Color it green.**

The United States of America

A Winner!

Read the passage. Then answer the questions.

She speeds along the ice. She jumps.
She twirls.

Michelle Kwan is one of the best skaters
of all time. She started skating when she
was five years old.

She competes in contests around the
world. She has won dozens of medals.

She is a winner!

1. Who is the passage about?

_____

2. What is the stated main idea?

_____

3. What else would you like to learn about this person?

_____

Assessment

Read the passage.

Look outside. Do you see some plants? We can eat some plants. Do you like lettuce and spinach? They are leaves from plants. Do you like carrots and potatoes? They are roots from plants. Do you like apples and blackberries? They are fruit from plants. All these plants are healthy foods.

Read the supporting details. Then write the stated main idea.

Stated Main Idea	Supporting Details
	leaves—lettuce and spinach roots—carrots and potatoes fruit—apples and blackberries healthy foods

Overview Identifying Supporting Details

Directions and Sample Answers for Activity Pages

Day 1	See "Provide a Real-World Example" below.
Day 2	Read the passages together. Discuss the stated main ideas. Then help students circle the supporting details in each passage. (**First:** how to use space tools; how to talk to people on Earth; how to eat and sleep in space; how to walk in space. **Second:** how big an animal was; if the animal walked on two or four feet; if the animal walked alone or in a group)
Day 3	Read and discuss each paragraph and stated main idea. Then help students write four details that support each main idea. (**First:** birds, squirrels, chipmunks, mice. **Second:** twigs, leaves, fruit, nuts.)
Day 4	Read and discuss each paragraph and stated main idea. Then help students locate and color the circle in front of each supporting detail from the paragraph. (**First:** don't understand what's happening; don't know where to go; don't know what to do. **Second:** pet's old bed and toys; pet's old food dish and water dish; extra attention and time to explore.)
Day 5	Read the passage together. Ask students to write the stated main idea in the first box on the graphic organizer. Then ask them to write the supporting details in the second box. Afterward, meet individually with students to discuss their results. Use their responses to plan further instruction and review. (**Stated main idea:** A mother polar bear takes good care of her cubs. **Supporting details:** digs a den to protect herself; stays with cubs for two years; keeps them warm; teaches them how to live in their icy home.)

Provide a Real-World Example

◆ Hand out the Day 1 activity page.

◆ **Say:** *Recently I listened to a speaker tell about recycling. He stated that people can recycle in many ways. Then he told about several different ways to recycle. What are some ways people can recycle?*

◆ Allow time for students to respond. Then ask them to complete the stated main idea on their page, draw a circle around the pictures that show ways to recycle, and draw or write about one other way to recycle. **Say:** *These different ways to recycle are details. The details support the main idea stated on the page.*

◆ Explain that students can also find supporting details when they read. Write the following on chart paper:

Identifying Supporting Details

See what the passage is about.

Find the sentence that tells the most important idea.

Find sentences that tell more information about the main idea.

Recycle!

Listen. Complete the stated main idea. Then circle the supporting details.

Stated Main Idea:

People can _____ in many ways.

Details

Draw another way to recycle.

Name _____

So Much to Learn

Read the passage.

Astronauts must learn to do many things. They must learn to use space tools. They must learn how to talk to people on Earth. They must learn how to eat and sleep in space. Learning how to walk in space is hard!

Stated Main Idea:

Astronauts must learn to do many things.

Circle the details that tell more about the main idea.

Read the passage.

Have you ever seen a fossil? Some fossils help us learn how animals lived long ago. They tell how big an animal was. They tell if the animal walked on two or four feet. They even tell if the animal walked alone or in a group.

Stated Main Idea:

Some fossils help us learn how animals lived long ago.

Circle the details that tell more about the main idea.

Animals in the Forest

Read each paragraph. Read the stated main idea.
Then write four details that support each main idea.

A forest is a busy place. Many animals live in the forest. Birds and squirrels build nests in the trees. Chipmunks and mice live on the forest floor.

Stated Main Idea: Many animals live in the forest.

Supporting Details:

_____

_____

_____

_____

Trees provide food for forest animals. Some animals eat twigs and leaves. Others eat fruit and nuts.

Stated Main Idea: Trees provide food for forest animals.

Supporting Details:

_____

_____

_____

Moving with Pets

Read each paragraph. Find the underlined stated main idea. Then color in the circle in front of each supporting detail you read in the paragraph.

Moving day can be hard on pets. They don't understand what's happening. They don't know where to go. They don't know what to do.

○ don't understand what's happening

○ don't like sleeping in a new place

○ don't know where to go

○ don't know what to do

Bring your pet's old bed, food dish, water dish, and toys. Give your pet time to explore. Give your pet extra attention. Doing these things will make your pet feel better.

○ pet's old bed and toys

○ pet's old food dish and water dish

○ extra treats and time to take a nap

○ extra attention and time to explore

Assessment

Read the passage.

A mother polar bear takes good care of her cubs. She digs a den to protect herself for the winter. In the spring, she comes out with new cubs. She stays with the cubs for two years. She keeps them warm. She teaches them how to live in their icy home.

Write the stated main idea in the first box. Then write the supporting details.

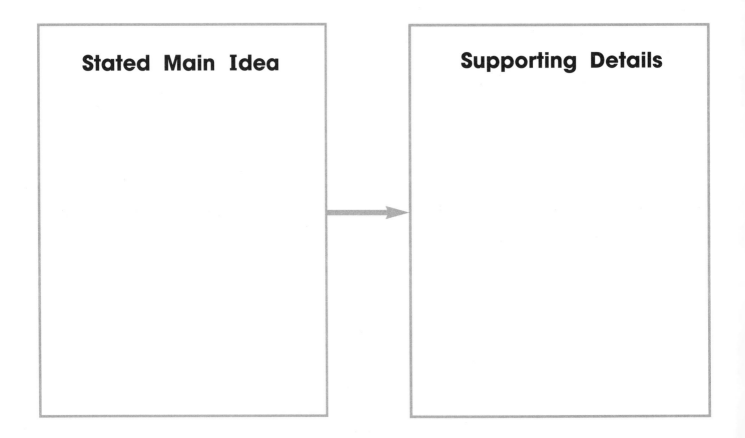

Stated Main Idea	Supporting Details

Overview   Summarizing Fiction

Directions and Sample Answers for Activity Pages

Day 1	See "Provide a Real-World Example" below.
Day 2	Discuss the pictures. Ask students to tell the story to a partner. Then help them select and circle the best summary. (A bee stung a bear who scared the bee's friends away.)
Day 3	Read and discuss the story. Help students underline the big ideas. Then help them complete the sentence to write a summary. (**Big ideas:** I get to swim. I get to quack, too. I get to swim. But I can't quack. You're a lucky duck! **Summary:** Swan thinks Duck is lucky because he can quack.)
Day 4	Read and discuss the story. Help students underline the big ideas. Then help them write a summary of the story. (**Big ideas:** Any day can be a holiday. All you need is a friend, a snack, and something fun to do. **Summary:** Nina and Grant made their own holiday.)
Day 5	Read the story together. Ask students to write the big ideas and summary on their graphic organizers. Afterward, meet individually with students to discuss their results. Use their responses to plan further instruction and review. (**Big ideas:** not happy; wanted to be different from other trees; sky gods became tired of yelling; turned tree upside down. **Summary:** The baobab tree wanted to be different, so the sky gods turned it upside down.)

Provide a Real-World Example

◆ Hand out the Day 1 activity page.

◆ **Say:** *Our days here at school are busy. What are some things we do each day?* Allow time for students to respond, and then **say:** *I can tell about our day in one sentence: At school, we learn important things and spend time with our friends. This sentence is a summary of our day at school.*

◆ Pair students and ask them to summarize one part of the school day, such as going to art class or eating in the cafeteria. Then ask them to look at the pictures on the page and summarize the story. If they have difficulty, offer some suggestions, such as *A boy and his dad had a busy evening while Mom was gone.*

◆ Explain that students can also summarize stories they read. Write the following on chart paper:

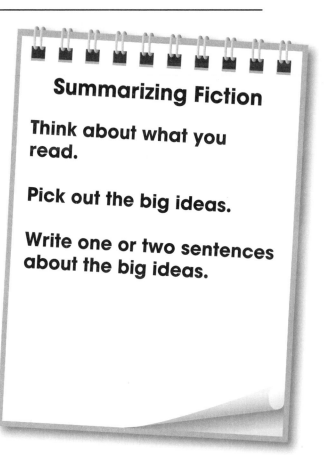

Summarizing Fiction

Think about what you read.

Pick out the big ideas.

Write one or two sentences about the big ideas.

Name _____

One Day

Look at the pictures on this page. Then summarize the story.

Unit 11 • Everyday Comprehension Intervention Activities Grade 2 • © 2010 Newmark Learning, LLC

Name _____

Three Friends

Look at the pictures. Tell the story to a partner.

Draw a circle around the best summary.

A bear scared a rabbit, mole, and bee. They ran away.

A bee stung a bear who scared the bee's friends away.

A rabbit and mole helped a bee scare away a bear.

Name _____

Lucky Duck

Read the story. Draw a line under the big ideas.

"Hi, Swan!" said Duck.

"Hello," said Swan. "Is it fun to be a duck?"

"Yes!" said Duck. "I get to swim. I get to quack, too!"

"I get to swim, too," said Swan. "But I can't quack!
You're a lucky duck!"

Complete the sentence to write a summary.

_____ thinks _____ is lucky because

he can _____.

Holiday!

Read the story. Draw a line under the big ideas.

"I love holidays!" said Nina.

"Today's not a holiday," said Grant.

"Any day can be a holiday," said Nina.

"All you need is a friend, a snack, and something fun to do."

"I see you have a snack and a game," said Grant.

"I have a friend, too!" said Nina.

"Holiday!" said Grant.

Write a summary of the story.

_____

_____

_____

_____

_____

Assessment

Read the story.

The baobab tree was not happy.

"I want to be different from the other trees.

I want to be taller and greener!

I want more flowers and fruit!"

The sky gods became tired of the baobab's yelling.

"We'll make you different," they said.

"We'll turn you upside down."

To this day, the baobab tree looks like it's upside down.

Write the big ideas. Then write a summary.

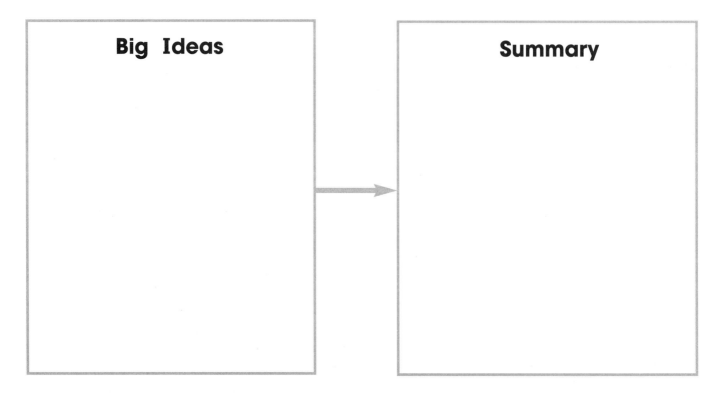

Big Ideas	Summary

Overview Summarizing Nonfiction

Directions and Sample Answers for Activity Pages

Day 1	See "Provide a Real-World Example" below.
Day 2	Ask students to tell a partner about the pictures. Then help them select and circle the best summary. (A caterpillar becomes a chrysalis and then becomes a butterfly.)
Day 3	Read and discuss the passage. Help students underline the big ideas. Then help them complete the sentence to write a summary. (**Big ideas:** live in a cold place called the Arctic; have fur to keep warm; fur is white to help them hide; wide, bumpy paws; help them walk on the ice. **Summary:** A polar bear's white fur and wide, bumpy paws help it live in the Arctic.)
Day 4	Read and discuss the passage. Help students underline the big ideas. Then help them write a summary of the passage. (**Big ideas:** Sometimes adding is too slow. It takes a while to think of 6 + 6 + 6 + 6. It only takes a second to think of 4 x 6. **Summary:** When you have equal groups, it is quicker to multiply than to add.)
Day 5	Read the passage together. Ask students to write the big ideas and summary on their graphic organizers. Afterward, meet individually with students to discuss their results. Use their responses to plan further instruction and review. (**Big ideas:** begins on land, strong winds, can hurt people, find a shelter, stay until the tornado is over. **Summary:** People should stay in a shelter to be safe from the strong winds of a tornado.)

Provide a Real-World Example

◆ Hand out the Day 1 activity page.

◆ **Say:** *I had a busy day last Saturday. It would take me an hour to tell you everything I did. Instead, I'll tell you a summary: I went shopping, ate dinner with my family, and saw a movie. This summary tells the most important things I did in one sentence.*

◆ Pair students and ask them to summarize what they did the previous evening. Then **say:** *Look at the pictures on the page. Summarize what the kids did one Saturday morning.* If students have difficulty, offer some suggestions, such as *Four kids had fun playing together at the park.*

◆ Explain that students can also summarize when they read. Write the following on chart paper:

Summarizing Nonfiction

Think about what you read.

Pick out the big ideas.

Write one or two sentences about the big ideas.

Name _____

The Playground

Look at the pictures. Then summarize what the kids did one Saturday morning.

Unit 12 • Everyday Comprehension Intervention Activities Grade 2 • © 2010 Newmark Learning, LLC

From Caterpillar to Butterfly

Tell a partner about the pictures.

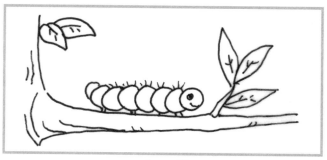

caterpillar

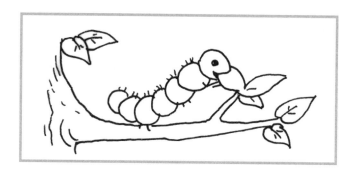

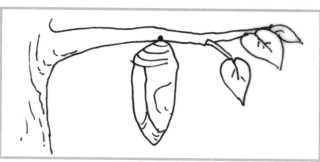

chrysalis

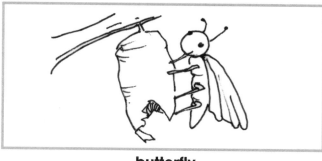

butterfly

Draw a circle around the best summary.

A butterfly is a type of caterpillar that lives in trees.

A caterpillar becomes a chrysalis and then becomes a butterfly.

A caterpillar eats leaves, but a butterfly flies.

Polar Bears

Read the passage. Draw a line under the big ideas.

Polar bears live in a cold place called the Arctic. Polars bears have fur to keep warm. The fur is white to help them hide in the snow and ice. Polar bears have wide, bumpy paws. These paws help them walk on the ice without slipping.

Complete the sentence to write a summary.

A polar bear's white _____ and wide, bumpy _____

help it live in the _____ .

Multiplication

Read the passage. Draw a line under the big ideas.

Adding is a handy skill.

Sometimes adding is too slow, though.

Think of four rows of desks.

Each row has six desks.

It takes a while to think of 6 + 6 + 6 + 6.

It only takes a second to think of 4 x 6!

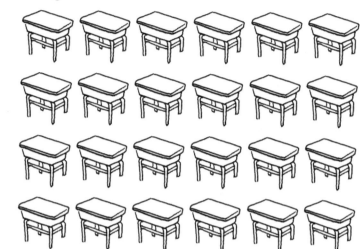

Write a summary of the passage.

_____

_____

_____

_____

Assessment

Read the passage.

A tornado begins over land.

It has strong winds.

The winds spin around in the shape
of a funnel.

A tornado can hurt people.

If you see a tornado coming, find a shelter.

Stay there until the tornado is over.

Write the big ideas. Then write a summary.

Big Ideas	Summary

Overview   Comparing and Contrasting in Fiction

Directions and Sample Answers for Activity Pages

Day 1	See "Provide a Real-World Example" below.
Day 2	Read and discuss the story. Then help students determine how the bears are alike and different. (**Alike:** both live with Mama; both are small and brown; both like to eat berries. **Different:** one is scared of the woods; one likes to climb trees.)
Day 3	Read and discuss the story. Then help students mark the chart by placing Xs in the appropriate columns to show how Jack and Joan are alike and different. (**Jack:** lives in the forest; plays; is happy; hears a loud noise; hides in a bush. **Joan:** lives in the forest; plays; is happy; hears a loud noise; keeps playing.)
Day 4	Read about Annie and Anya together. Discuss. Then help students circle the best answers. (**1:** Anya. **2:** both. **3:** both. **4:** Annie. **5:** Anya. **6:** both.)
Day 5	Read the story together. Ask students to write how Ralph and Ruff are alike and different on their graphic organizers. Afterward, meet individually with students to discuss their results. Use their responses to plan further instruction and review. (**Ralph:** black and white; chases balls. **Ruff:** brown; sleeps in the sun. **Both:** go for walks; nice; Meggie loves them.)

Provide a Real-World Example

◆ Hand out the Day 1 activity page.

◆ **Say:** *My friend lives in an apartment. She takes an elevator to her home. Another friend lives in a house. It is all on one level. Both of these places are homes. They are both places where families live.*

◆ Ask students to look at the pictures of the apartment and house. **Say:** *We can compare these two homes. How are the homes alike?* Discuss. Then **say:** *We can contrast these two homes. How are the homes different?* Discuss.

◆ Ask students to draw a picture of their own home or the home of a family member or friend. Then invite them to share how this home is the same as and different from the homes in the pictures.

◆ Explain that students can also compare and contrast things when they read stories. Write the following on chart paper:

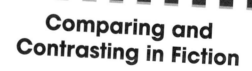

Comparing and Contrasting in Fiction

Look at the pictures.

Think about the words.

See how things are alike. Look for words like *alike*, *too*, and *both*.

See how things are different. Look for words like *different*, *one*, and *but*.

Homes

Compare and contrast these two homes.

How are they alike? How are they different?

Draw a picture of your home or the home of a family member or friend.

How is this home the same as the homes above? How is this home different?

Baby Bears

Read the story.

Mama smiled at Ben and Bernie.

"Come, my small, brown bears.
Let's go to the woods for berries."

"Yum!" said Ben. "I like berries!

"I do, too!" said Bernie.

Bernie stayed close to Mama.

"I'm scared of the woods," he said.

But Ben went exploring. "Look! I climbed a tree!" he called.

How are Ben and Bernie alike? Draw a circle around the best answers.

They both live with Mama.

They are both small and brown.

They both like to eat berries.

They are both scared of the woods.

They both like to climb trees.

How are Ben and Bernie different? Draw a circle around the best answers.

One lives with Mama Bear.

One is small and brown.

One likes to eat berries.

One is scared of the woods.

One likes to climb trees.

Two Happy Chipmunks

Read the story. Then mark the chart.

Jack and Joan played in the forest.

"This is a great day!" they said.

Suddenly, they heard a loud noise.

"What was that?" Jack cried. "I'm going
to hide in this bush!"

"Not me! " said Joan. "I'm going to keep playing!"

	Jack	Joan
This chipmunk lives in the forest.		
This chipmunk plays.		
This chipmunk is happy.		
This chipmunk hears a loud noise.		
This chipmunk hides in a bush.		
This chipmunk keeps playing.		

    Unit 13 • Everyday Comprehension Intervention Activities Grade 2 • © 2010 Newmark Learning, LLC

Annie and Anya

Read about Annie and Anya.

Annie and Anya are best friends.
They draw and paint together. They
jump rope, too.

But Annie likes to be by herself sometimes.
She goes to her room to read.

Anya likes to spend time with her family.
She visits her grandmother every
afternoon.

Draw a circle around the best answer.

1. Who spends the most time with family?   Annie   Anya   Both

2. Who likes to jump rope?   Annie   Anya   Both

3. Who has a best friend?   Annie   Anya   Both

4. Who spends the most time reading?   Annie   Anya   Both

5. Who visits her grandmother every day?   Annie   Anya   Both

6. Who likes to draw and paint?   Annie   Anya   Both

Assessment

Read the story.

"Are these your dogs?" asked Ben.

"Yes," said Meggie. "The black-and-white one is Ralph.

He loves to chase balls and go for walks.

The brown one is Ruff.

He likes to walk, too. But he mostly sleeps in the sun."

"Your dogs are nice," said Ben.

"Yes!" said Meggie. "I love them both!"

Write how Ralph and Ruff are alike and different.

Ralph	Ralph and Ruff	Ruff

Overview Comparing and Contrasting in Nonfiction

Directions and Sample Answers for Activity Pages

Day 1	See "Provide a Real-World Example" below.
Day 2	Read and discuss the passage. Then help students determine how a robin and a parakeet are alike and different. (**Alike:** birds; have feathers and beaks. **Different:** one lives outdoors; one builds a nest; one lives in a cage; one is a pet)
Day 3	Read and discuss the passage. Then help students mark the chart by placing Xs in the appropriate columns to show how Venus and Saturn are alike and different. (**Venus:** is in the solar system; is small; travels around the sun; has no moons. **Saturn:** is in the solar system; has lots of moons; travels around the sun; has rings around it; is giant.)
Day 4	Read and discuss the passage. Then help students circle the best answers. (**1:** both. **2:** rural area. **3:** urban area. **4:** both. **5:** rural area. **6:** both. **7:** urban area. **8:** both.)
Day 5	Read the passage together. Ask students to write how spring and summer are alike and different on their graphic organizers. Afterward, meet individually with students to discuss their results. Use their responses to plan further instruction and review. (**Spring:** warm. **Summer:** hot; people swim at the beach. **Both:** seasons; flowers; people go walking.)

Provide a Real-World Example

◆ Hand out the Day 1 activity page.

◆ **Say:** *Many people enjoy sports. One of my friends likes to play tennis. She uses a racket to hit a ball over a net. My cousin plays baseball. He hits a ball, too, but he uses a bat. Tennis and baseball are both sports. We can compare these two sports by thinking about ways they are alike. We can contrast the two sports by thinking about the ways they are different.*

◆ Ask students to look at the pictures of people playing soccer and basketball. **Ask:** *How are these two sports the same? How are these two sports different?* Repeat the activity with the pictures of people swimming and rowing.

◆ Invite students to name two other sports to compare and contrast. Then explain that students can also compare and contrast things when they read. Write the following on chart paper:

Comparing and Contrasting in Nonfiction

Look at the pictures.

Think about the words.

See how things are alike.
Look for words like *alike*, *both*, and *too*.

See how things are different.
Look for words like *different*, *one*, and *but*.

Sports We Play

Look at the pictures in each row. How are these sports the same? How are they different?

Robins and Parakeets

Read the passage.

Parakeets and robins are both birds. They both have
feathers and beaks. But robins live outdoors. They fly up into
trees. They build nests there. Most parakeets live in cages.
They are pets.

How are a robin and parakeet alike? Draw a circle around the best answers.

They are both birds.

They both have feathers and beaks.

They both live outdoors.

They both build nests.

They both live in cages.

They are both pets.

How are a robin and parakeet different? Draw a circle around the best answers.

One is a bird.

One has feathers and a beak.

One lives outdoors.

One builds a nest.

One lives in a cage.

One is a pet.

Write one more way robins and parakeets are alike.

_____

Write one more way robins and parakeets are different.

_____

Two Planets

Read the passage. Then mark the chart.

Our solar system has eight planets. All the planets travel around the sun.

One planet in the solar system is Venus. Venus is a small planet. It has no moons.

Saturn is a planet in the solar system, too. But Saturn is a giant planet. It has rings around it. Saturn has lots of moons.

	Venus	Saturn
This planet is in the solar system.		
This planet has lots of moons.		
This planet is small.		
This planet travels around the sun.		
This planet has rings around it.		
This planet has no moons.		
This planet is giant.		

   Unit 14 • Everyday Comprehension Intervention Activities Grade 2 • © 2010 Newmark Learning, LLC

Urban or Rural?

Read the passage.

People live in urban areas and rural areas. Urban areas and rural areas both have homes and schools. They both have cars, too.

Urban areas have streets and tall buildings. But rural areas have roads and farms.

Would you like to live in an urban area or a rural area?

Draw a circle around the best answer.

1. You see people here.	urban area	rural area	both
2. You see roads here.	urban area	rural area	both
3. You see tall buildings here.	urban area	rural area	both
4. You see homes here.	urban area	rural area	both
5. You see farms here.	urban area	rural area	both
6. You see schools here.	urban area	rural area	both
7. You see sidewalks here.	urban area	rural area	both
8. You see cars here.	urban area	rural area	both

Assessment

Read the passage.

Spring and summer are both seasons. The air turns warm in the spring, but summers can be very hot.

Flowers bloom in the spring. Many of them keep blooming all summer.

People go for walks in the spring. People go walking in the summer, too. People swim at the beach in the summer.

Write how spring and summer are alike and different.

Spring	Spring and Summer	Summer

Overview Identifying Cause and Effect in Fiction

Directions and Sample Answers for Activity Pages

Day 1	See "Provide a Real-World Example" below.
Day 2	Read and discuss the sentences and pictures. Then help students draw or write an effect for each cause. (**Zoe:** she will build a snowman. **Rabbit:** the tower will fall over.)
Day 3	Read and discuss the sentences and pictures. Then help students draw or write a cause for each effect. (**Calvin:** he jumped in a puddle. **Max Monkey:** his friend ate a banana.)
Day 4	Read and discuss the poem. Explain that some stories have more than one cause and effect. Then help students complete each effect. (**First:** The birds were noisy. **Second:** Mama made worm pie. **Third:** The birds were quiet. **Fourth:** The birds said, "Thank you.")
Day 5	Read the story together. Ask students to write one of the causes and effects on their graphic organizers. Afterward, meet individually with students to discuss their results. Use their responses to plan further instruction and review. (**Cause:** Bear wanted to start the movie. **Effect:** He called to Father and Sister. **Cause:** Bear called to Father and Sister. **Effect:** They came running. **Cause:** Father and Sister came. **Effect:** Bear finally got to watch the movie.)

Provide a Real-World Example

◆ Hand out the Day 1 activity page.

◆ **Say:** *Once I dropped a cup on the kitchen floor. It broke into many pieces. A cause is why something happens. What caused the cup to break?* Allow time for students to respond. Then **say:** *An effect is what happens. What was the effect when I dropped the cup?*

◆ Write the words **cause** and **effect** on the board. Ask students to look at the pictures and write **cause** or **effect** under each picture as you discuss.

◆ Explain that they can also find causes and effects when they read stories. Write the following on chart paper:

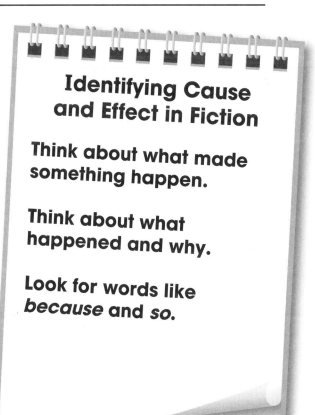

Identifying Cause and Effect in Fiction

Think about what made something happen.

Think about what happened and why.

Look for words like *because* **and** *so.*

In the Kitchen

Look at each row of pictures. Then label each picture *cause* or *effect*.

_____

_____

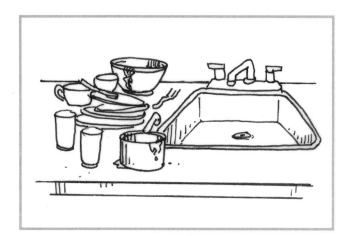

_____

_____

_____

_____

So . . .

Read the sentences. Look at the pictures.

Then draw or write an effect for each cause.

Zoe loves to play in the snow, so . . .

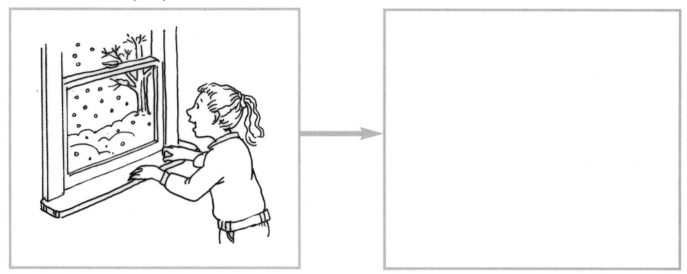

Rabbit's tower is getting too high, so . . .

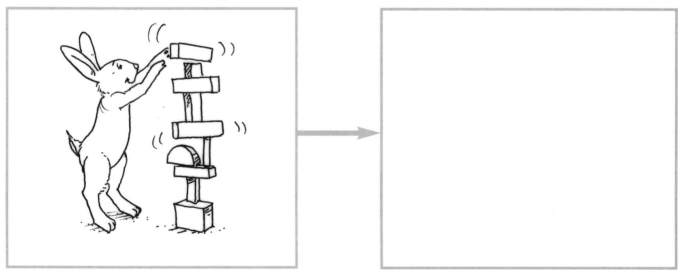

Because . . .

Read the sentences. Look at the pictures.

Then draw or write a cause for each effect.

Calvin is wet because . . .

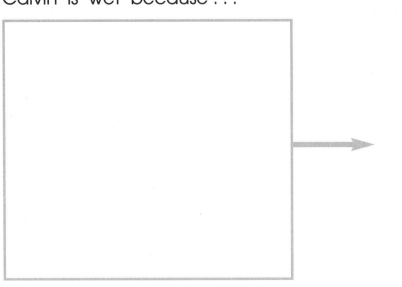 

Max Monkey found a banana peel because . . .

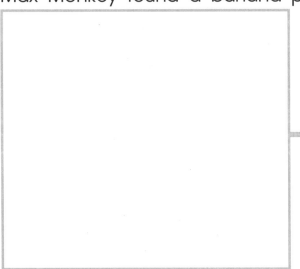  

Unit 15 • Everyday Comprehension Intervention Activities Grade 2 • © 2010 Newmark Learning, LLC

Three Noisy Birds

Read the poem.

Three noisy birds.

"We're hungry," they cry.

Three noisy birds.

"Mama went good-bye."

Three noisy birds.

"Mama made worm pie!"

Three quiet birds.

"Thank you," they sigh.

Sometimes a story has many causes and effects. Complete each effect.

Cause: The birds were hungry.

Effect: The birds were _____.

Cause: The birds were hungry.

Effect: Mama made _____.

Cause: Mama made worm pie.

Effect: The birds were _____.

Cause: Mama made worm pie.

Effect: The birds said _____.

Assessment

Read the story.

It was movie night.

"May we start, Mama?" Bear asked.

"You know you must wait for everyone," Mama answered.

Bear called to his father. "Movie time!"

Father came running.

Bear called to his sister. "Movie time!"

Sister came running.

They all sat on the sofa.

"Movie time!" said Bear.

Write one of the causes and effects.

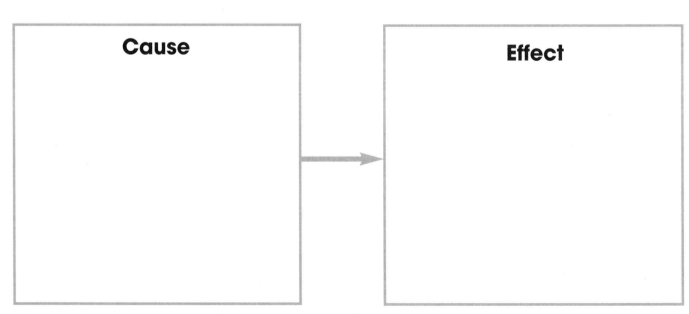

Cause	Effect

Overview Identifying Cause and Effect in Nonfiction

Directions and Sample Answers for Activity Pages

Day 1	See "Provide a Real-World Example" below.
Day 2	Read and discuss the sentences and pictures. Then help students draw or write an effect for each cause. (**Circle:** trace around a bowl or other round object. **Square:** use a ruler or other measuring tool.)
Day 3	Read and discuss the sentences and pictures. Then help students draw or write a cause for each effect. (**Grocery store:** they need food to eat at home. **Recycling center:** they have collected cans, bottles, and paper at home.)
Day 4	Read and discuss the passage. Explain that some passages have more than one cause and effect. Then help students complete each effect. (**First:** The author says fish are busy creatures. **Second:** Fish swim. **Third:** Fish swim. **Fourth:** The fish hide. **Fifth:** The fish go back to swimming.)
Day 5	Read the passage together. Ask students to write one of the causes and effects on their graphic organizers. Afterward, meet individually with students to discuss their results. Use their responses to plan further instruction and review. (**Cause:** Different-size wheels made it hard for bikes to go. **Effect:** People started making the wheels the same size. **Cause:** Bikes had no pedals. **Effect:** Riders had to use their feet to go. **Cause:** People wanted bikes to be easier to ride. **Effect:** People started making pedals.)

Provide a Real-World Example

◆ Hand out the Day 1 activity page.

◆ **Say:** *My friend loves fresh vegetables. Because of this, she made a garden in her yard so she can grow her own vegetables. A cause is why something happens. What caused my friend to make a garden?* Allow time for students to respond. Then **say:** *An effect is what happens. What is the effect of my friend's love for fresh vegetables?*

◆ Write the words **cause** and **effect** on the board. Ask students to look at the pictures and write **cause** or **effect** under each picture as you discuss.

◆ Explain that students can also find causes and effects when they read. Write the following on chart paper:

Identifying Cause and Effect in Nonfiction

Think about what made something happen.

Think about what happened and why.

Look for words like *because* **and** *so.*

In the Yard

Look at each row of pictures. Then label each picture *cause* or *effect*.

_____   _____

_____   _____

_____   _____

Drawing Shapes

Read the sentences. Look at the pictures. Then draw or write an effect for each cause.

It is hard to draw a perfect circle, so many people . . .

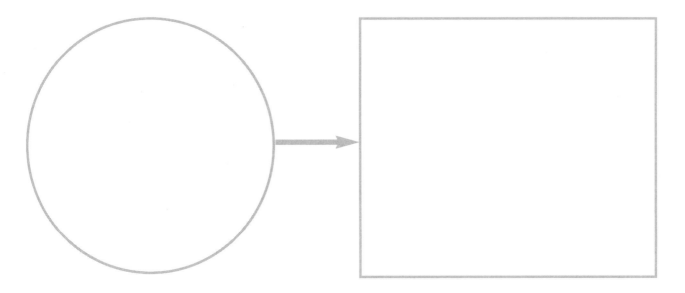

The sides of a square are the same length, so many people . . .

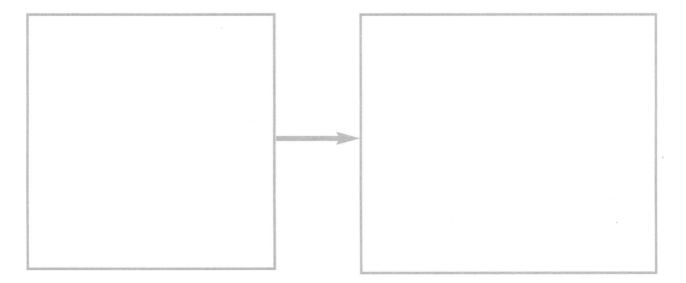

Running Errands

Read the sentences. Look at the pictures. Then draw or write a cause for each effect.

People go to the grocery store because . . .

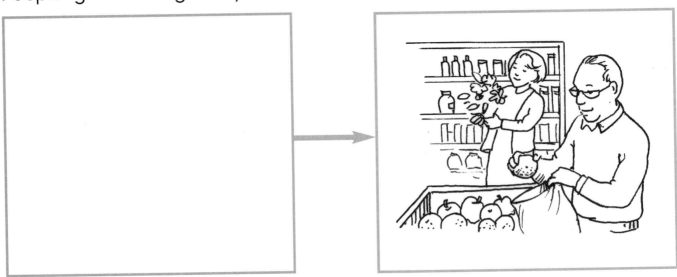

People go to the recycling center because . . .

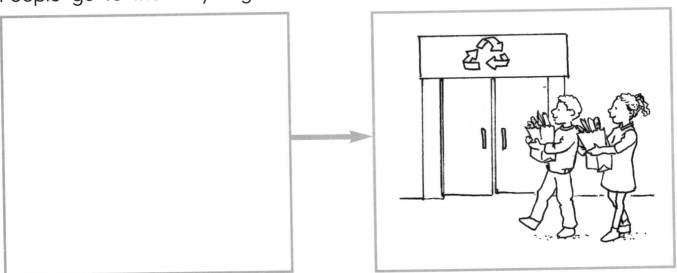

Busy Fish

Read the passage.

Fish are busy creatures. They are often on the go.

Fish swim to get from place to place.

They swim so they can find food, too.

Sometimes fish hide because a bigger fish is coming.

When the big fish is gone, they can go back to swimming.

Sometimes a passage has many causes and effects. Complete each effect.

Cause: Fish are often on the go.

Effect: The author says fish are _____.

Cause: Fish need to get from place to place.

Effect: Fish _____.

Cause: Fish need to find food.

Effect: Fish _____.

Cause: A bigger fish is coming.

Effect: The fish _____.

Cause: The big fish goes away.

Effect: The fish _____.

Assessment

Read the passage.

Long ago, some bikes had one big wheel and one small wheel. This made it hard for them to go. So people started making the wheels the same size.

Other bikes had no pedals. Riders had to use their feet to go. Then people started making pedals because they wanted bikes to be easier to ride.

Write one of the causes and effects.

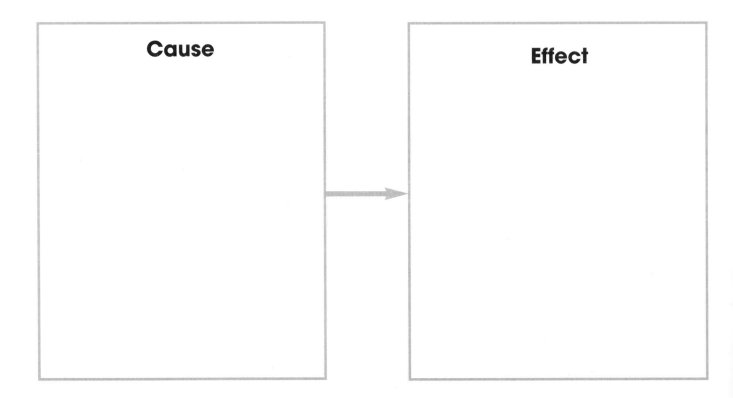

Cause	**Effect**

Overview Making Inferences in Fiction

Directions and Sample Answers for Activity Pages

Day 1	See "Provide a Real-World Example" below.
Day 2	Discuss the pictures. Then help students circle the best inference for each picture. (It is almost dinner time. The girl is going to a birthday party. The game is over.)
Day 3	Read and discuss the story. Then help students write their ideas in the boxes. (**Clues:** A model airplane breaks easily. Dean wants Dad to put it on a high shelf. **Already know:** Babies break things. A baby cannot reach a high shelf. **Inference:** Dean has a baby brother/baby sister/little brother/little sister.)
Day 4	Read and discuss the story. Then help students circle the best answer to each question. (**Clue:** Rob has been late two times. **Already know:** Some people are usually late. **Inference:** Rob will be late next time, too.)
Day 5	Read the story together. Ask students to write clues from the story and what they already know about the clues. Then ask them to make an inference about where Raphael and Jovan are going. Afterward, meet individually with students to discuss their results. Use their responses to plan further instruction and review. (**Clues:** paint; wish we could have class every day. **Already know:** Kids paint in art class. Most kids don't have art class every day. **Inference:** The kids are going to art class.)

Provide a Real-World Example

◆ Hand out the Day 1 activity page.

◆ **Say:** *Imagine I brought a suitcase to school today. The suitcase is a clue. You already know something about suitcases, too. Think about the clue and what you already know. Can you make a good guess, or inference, about what I will do after school?*

◆ Allow time for students to discuss their ideas and then complete the sentence. They should infer that you will leave on a trip. However, point out that an inference isn't always correct. For example, you could be taking some old clothes to a thrift store in the suitcase.

◆ Repeat the process with the other items on the page. Then explain that students can also make inferences when they read stories. Write the following on chart paper:

Making Inferences in Fiction

Find clues in the pictures.

Find clues in the words.

Think about what you already know.

Try to figure out what the author does not state.

My Teacher Will . . .

Listen. Then complete each inference.

My teacher will _____.

My teacher will _____.

My teacher will _____.

My teacher will _____.

Picture Clues

Draw a circle around the best inference for each picture.

It is almost dinner time.

It is time for bed.

The girl is going to school.

The girl is going to a birthday party.

The game is over.

It is time for the game to start.

Name _____

Dean's Model Airplane

Read the story. Then write your ideas in the boxes.

"I finished my model airplane!" said Dean.

"I like it," said Dad.

"Be careful, though. Model airplanes break easily."

"True," said Dean. "Will you put it on a high shelf?"

I know from the story that . . .

I already know . . .

I can make an inference.

Dean has a _____.

Where's Rob?

Read the story.

Deb and Patrick stood in front of the library. Deb looked at her watch.

"Where's Rob?" she asked. "He was supposed to be here by now."

"He was late last time we met, too," said Patrick.

"I'm glad we only have one more meeting after this," said Deb. "Then our class project will be done."

Which clue is in the story? Draw a circle around the best answer.

Rob has been late two times.

Rob does not have a watch.

What do you already know? Draw a circle around the best answer.

Kids do not like to do class projects.

Some people are usually late.

Which is the best inference? Draw a circle around the best answer.

The kids will ask the teacher for a new project.

Rob will be late next time, too.

Assessment

Read the story.

Raphael and Jovan walked down the hall.

"Ms. Penn said we will paint today," Raphael said.

"I wish we could have Ms. Penn's class every day!" Jovan exclaimed.

Write the clues from the story. Write what you already know.
Then write an inference.

Clues	What I Already Know

Inference

Overview Making Inferences in Nonfiction

Directions and Sample Answers for Activity Pages

Day 1	See "Provide a Real-World Example" below.
Day 2	Discuss the pictures. Then help students make an inference about what they might do on each page and draw a circle around the best title. (**1:** Adding Apples. **2:** Subtracting Apples. **3:** Multiplying Apples. **4:** Dividing Apples.)
Day 3	Read and discuss the passage. Then help students write their ideas in the boxes and draw a picture to go with their inference. (**Evidence:** Ducks have feet that are wide and flat. Webbed feet help ducks swim. **Already know:** Swimming flippers look like duck feet. **Inference:** People invented swimming flippers after looking at duck feet.)
Day 4	Read and discuss the journal entry. Then help students circle the best answer to each question. (**Evidence:** Some girls went to the library. **Already know:** Kids who like to read often go to the library. **Inference:** The girls like to read.)
Day 5	Read the passage together. Ask students to write evidence from the passage and what they already know about the evidence. Then ask them to make an inference about what people might do with state quarters. Afterward, meet individually with students to discuss their results. Use their responses to plan further instruction and review. (**Evidence:** Every state has a special quarter. **Already know:** The United States has fifty states. Many people like to collect coins. **Inference:** Many people have all fifty state quarters.)

Provide a Real-World Example

◆ Hand out the Day 1 activity page.

◆ **Say:** *Yesterday I saw some students in the hallway carrying lunches. The lunches are a clue. You already know something about lunches, too. Think about the clue and what you already know. Can you make a good guess, or inference, about where the kids were going?*

◆ Allow time for students to discuss their ideas and then complete the sentence. They should infer that the students were going to the cafeteria. However, point out that an inference isn't always correct. For example, the students may have been leaving for a field trip.

◆ Repeat the process with the other pictures on the page. Then explain that students can also make inferences when they read. Write the following on chart paper:

Making Inferences in Nonfiction

Find evidence in the pictures.

Find evidence in the words.

Think about what you already know.

Try to figure out what the author does not state.

Where Are They Going?

Listen. Then complete each inference.

The kids are going

_____.

The kids are going

_____.

The kids are going

_____.

The kids are going

_____.

Apple Math

Look at the pictures from a math book. Make an inference about what you might do on each page. Then draw a circle around the best title.

1.

Adding Apples   Subtracting Apples

2.

Adding Apples   Subtracting Apples

3.

Subtracting Apples   Multiplying Apples

4.

Adding Apples   Dividing Apples

Duck Feet

Read the passage. Then write your ideas in the boxes.
Draw a picture to go with your inference.

Ducks have feet that are wide and flat.

Feet like this are called webbed feet.

Webbed feet help ducks swim.

How can learning about duck feet
help people swim?

I know from the passage that . . .

I already know . . .

I can make an inference.

People invented _____ after looking
at duck feet.

Unit 18 • Everyday Comprehension Intervention Activities Grade 2 • © 2010 Newmark Learning, LLC

My Journal

Some people write in journals every day. Read the journal entry.

Saturday, June 20

I went to the library this
morning. I saw Randa and Ali.
Randa got a book about horses.
Ali got one about sports. I got
a story book. Then we sat down
in a quiet corner to read.

What evidence is in the journal entry? Draw a circle around the best answer.

Some girls went to the library.

There were many people in the library.

What do you already know? Draw a circle around the best answer.

Libraries do not have books about horses.

Kids who like to read often go to the library.

Which is the best inference? Draw a circle around the best answer.

The girls all like to read.

The girls all like sports.

Assessment

Read the passage.

Did you know that every state in the United States has a special quarter?

The first state to have a quarter was Delaware.

This quarter came out in January 1999.

The last state to have a quarter was Hawaii.

This quarter came out in November 2008.

Write the evidence from the story. Write what you already know. Then write an inference

Evidence	What I Already Know

Inference

Overview Drawing Conclusions in Fiction

Directions and Sample Answers for Activity Pages

Day 1	See "Provide a Real-World Example" below.
Day 2	Read about each character. Use the clues to draw a conclusion. Then draw a line to the right character. (**1:** princess. **2:** owl. **3:** boy.)
Day 3	Read and discuss the story. Help students circle the best conclusion. Then help them circle the clues they used from the story. (**Conclusion:** Nan and Chet are working on a project at school. **Clues:** idea; have a plan; work in the classroom; teacher; draw the pictures; make the model; down the hall to the library; supplies.)
Day 4	Read and discuss the story. Help students write a conclusion about Sheera. Then help them draw a line under the clues they used from the story. (**Conclusion:** Sheera decided her sidewalk was not a safe place to play. **Clues:** They saw broken glass. Let's NOT play on my sidewalk. Let's play on yours.)
Day 5	Read the story together. Ask students to write clues from the story on their graphic organizers. Then ask them to write a conclusion. Afterward, meet individually with students to discuss their results. Use their responses to plan further instruction and review. (**Clues:** lunch; camera; whole class; teacher; dad going; mom going; bus. **Conclusion:** Kendra's class is going on a field trip.)

Provide a Real-World Example

◆ Hand out the Day 1 activity page.

◆ **Say:** *Think about people you know who have hobbies. Some people collect things. Some people draw or paint. Some people sing or dance. Some people make things. Some people play sports. People spend time on their hobbies. They spend money on their hobbies. They talk about their hobbies, too. All these things are clues. You can use the clues to figure out that people choose something they like to do for a hobby.*

◆ Tell students that using several clues to figure something out is called drawing a conclusion. Ask them to draw a picture of themselves or someone else enjoying a hobby. Then help them fill in the clues about the hobby. One at a time, ask students to read their clues to the class. Once the class draws the correct conclusion about the hobby, invite the student to share the picture.

◆ Explain that they can also draw conclusions when they read stories. Write the following on chart paper:

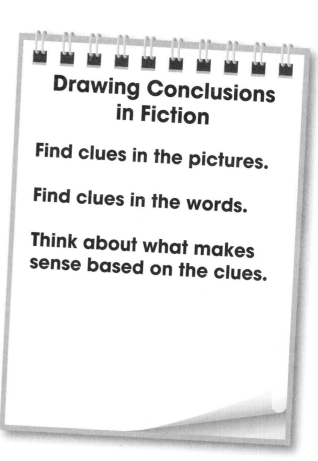

Drawing Conclusions in Fiction

Find clues in the pictures.

Find clues in the words.

Think about what makes sense based on the clues.

Hobbies

Draw a picture of someone enjoying a hobby. Then write clues about the hobby.

Clues:

1. This person spends time on _____.

2. This person spends money on _____.

3. This person talks about _____.

What a Character!

Read about each character. Use the clues to draw a conclusion. Then draw a line to the right character.

1. I live in a castle.

   I have a large kingdom.

   My brother is a prince.

   We have a pet dragon.

2. I live in a forest.

   I can fly.

   I stay up at night.

   Animals come to me for help.

3. I live in an apartment.

   I'm a good big brother.

   I play soccer with my friends.

   I want to write a book someday.

Nan's Plan

Read the story.

"I have an idea," said Nan. "I will draw the pictures, and you can make the model."

"Great!" said Chet. "Now we have a plan."

Nan frowned. "Should we work in the classroom? Or should we go down the hall to the library?"

"Let's work here," Chet replied. "Our teacher has the best supplies."

Which is the best conclusion? Draw a circle around your answer.

Nan and Chet are working on a project at school.

Nan is helping Chet make a model at the library.

Which clues for the conclusion are in the story?
Draw a circle around your answers.

idea	draw the pictures
after school	make the model
have a plan	work at home
work in the classroom	markers
scissors	down the hall to the library
teacher	supplies

 Unit 19 • Everyday Comprehension Intervention Activities Grade 2 • © 2010 Newmark Learning, LLC

Hopscotch

Read the story.

"Let's play hopscotch!" said Sheera.

"Where shall we play?" asked Allie.

"Let's play on my sidewalk," said Sheera.

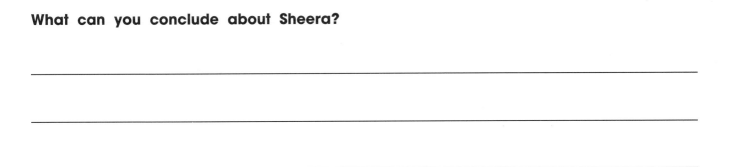

Sheera and Allie went to the sidewalk.

They saw broken glass.

"Let's NOT play on my sidewalk," said Sheera.

"Let's play on yours!"

What can you conclude about Sheera?

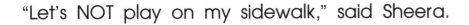

_____

_____

Draw a line under the clues you used to draw a conclusion.

Assessment

Read the story.

Kendra joined the other kids waiting outside the school.

"I remembered my lunch and camera!" she said.

She looked around. Her whole class was there. So was her teacher.

"My dad is going with us!" said Will.

"So is my mom!" said Callie.

A big bus pulled up.

"Away we go!" said Kendra.

Write the clues from the story. Then write a conclusion.

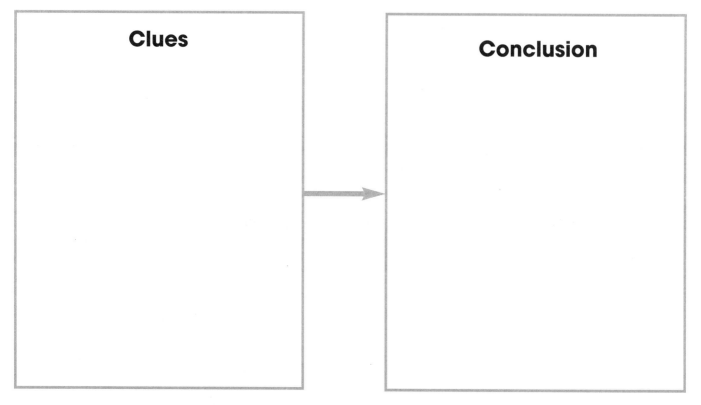

Clues	Conclusion

Overview Drawing Conclusions in Nonfiction

Directions and Sample Answers for Activity Pages

Day 1	See "Provide a Real-World Example" below.
Day 2	Read and discuss the sentences and pictures. Then help students draw a circle around the best conclusion for each set. (**First:** Some people make places to play with wood. **Second:** Some things made of cloth are not clothes.)
Day 3	Read and discuss the story. Help students circle the best conclusion. Then help them circle the evidence they used from the story. (**Conclusion:** Taking turns is a good rule at a park. **Evidence:** park rules; swinging; get off the swing; not on signs; waiting a long time; boy can have a turn.)
Day 4	Read and discuss the story. Help students write a conclusion about frogs. Then help them draw a line under the evidence they used from the passage. (**Conclusion:** Most people have seen a frog. **Evidence:** Frogs live in most places on Earth. They live on water and on land. Many people notice frogs when they jump.)
Day 5	Read the passage together. Ask students to write evidence from the passage on their graphic organizers. Then ask them to write a conclusion. Afterward, meet individually with students to discuss their results. Use their responses to plan further instruction and review. (**Evidence:** fly kites for fun; fly kites to tell about the new year; have "Kite Day"; fly kites all day long. **Conclusion:** People everywhere enjoy flying kites.)

Provide a Real-World Example

◆ Hand out the Day 1 activity page.

◆ **Say:** *Imagine you are looking at a person. She is at the wheel of a yellow bus. Kids are getting on the bus. She is smiling and greeting the kids by name. All these things you see are evidence. You can use the evidence to figure out that the woman is a school bus driver.*

◆ Tell students that using several pieces of evidence to figure something out is called drawing a conclusion. Ask them to draw a picture of another adult at work. Then help them fill in the evidence about the person's job. One at a time, ask students to read their evidence to the class. Once the class draws the correct conclusion about the job, invite the student to share the picture.

◆ Explain that students can also draw conclusions when they read. Write the following on chart paper:

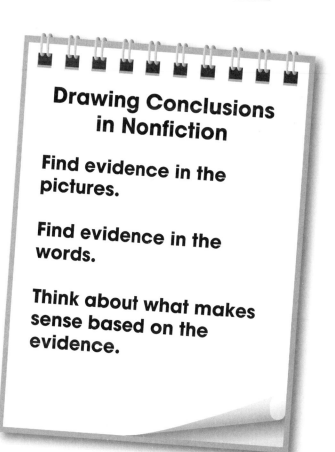

Drawing Conclusions in Nonfiction

Find evidence in the pictures.

Find evidence in the words.

Think about what makes sense based on the evidence.

What Is the Job?

Draw a picture of someone doing a job. Then list some evidence about the person's job.

Evidence:

1. This person _____.

2. This person _____.

3. This person _____.

Making Things

Read the sentences. Look at each group of pictures. Think about the evidence in the words and pictures. Then draw a circle around the best conclusion.

People make many things with wood.

 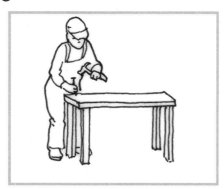 

Conclusion:

Some people make places to play with wood.

People only make houses with wood.

People make many things with cloth.

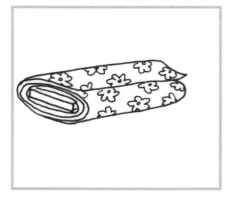  

Conclusion:

People can wear anything made from cloth.

Some things made of cloth are not clothes.

Park Rules

Read the passage.

Parks have rules.

A sign may say, "Put your trash in the can."

A sign may say, "Please don't pick the flowers."

Some park rules are not on signs, though.

You are swinging. A boy has been waiting a long time.

You can get off the swing. Then the boy can have a turn.

Which is the best conclusion? Draw a circle around your answer.

All park rules should be on signs.

Taking turns is a good rule at a park.

What evidence for the conclusion is in the story? Draw a circle around your answers.

park rules   not on signs

swinging   pick the flowers

pick up trash   waiting a long time

get off the swing   boy can have a turn

Frogs All Around

Read the passage.

Frogs live in most places on Earth.

They live on water and on land.

Frogs come in all sizes.

Some tree frogs are the size of a paper clip.

An African giant frog can weigh ten pounds!

Many people notice frogs when they jump.

One of the best jumpers is the common bullfrog.

What is one thing you can conclude about frogs?

_____

_____

_____

Draw a line under the clues you used to draw your conclusion.

Assessment

Read the passage.

A kite flies in the wind at the end of string.

A kite can be any shape. It can be any size.

Most people fly kites for fun.

In some places, people fly kites to tell about the new year.

In other places, people have "Kite Day." They fly kites all day long!

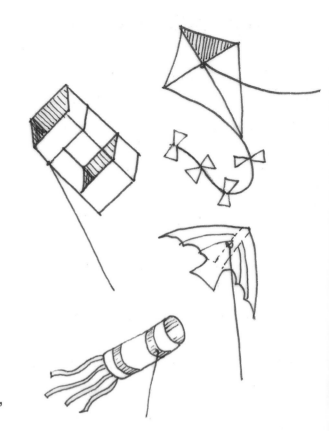

Write the evidence from the passage. Then write a conclusion.

Evidence	Conclusion

Overview Evaluating Author's Purpose in Fiction

Directions and Sample Answers for Activity Pages

Day 1	See "Provide a Real-World Example" below.
Day 2	Read and discuss the back-cover blurbs. Then help students circle the author's purpose for each one and draw a picture that might be in one of the books. (entertain readers by telling some scary stories; entertain readers with a story about forest animals)
Day 3	Read and discuss the riddles. Then help students complete the sentence about the author's purpose and draw a picture about one of the riddles. (The author probably wants to entertain readers with funny riddles.)
Day 4	Read and discuss the story. Then help students write the author's purpose and underline the clues in the story. (**Author's purpose:** to entertain readers with a tall tale. **Clues:** The moon ran away. Out came Big Bob's lasso. He swung it in the air. He grabbed that moon. He pulled it back. He tied it tight.)
Day 5	Read the poem together. Ask students to write clues about the author's purpose on the graphic organizer. Then ask them to record the author's purpose. Afterward, meet individually with students to discuss their results. Use their responses to plan further instruction and review. (**Clues:** The author talks about everything that is going wrong that day. The author says, "Who made this day up, anyway?" **Author's purpose:** to entertain readers with a silly poem.)

Provide a Real-World Example

Evaluating Author's Purpose in Fiction

Find clues in the pictures.

Find clues in the words.

Think like the author.

Think about how the author tries to entertain.

◆ Hand out the Day 1 activity page.

◆ **Say:** *I have always liked to watch singing and dancing. So I watched a movie with lots of singing and dancing last night. It had many surprising details. It made me laugh. From these clues, I could tell that the singers, dancers, and actors all wanted to entertain the audience.*

◆ Ask students to Think/Pair/Share a movie they think is entertaining. Then **say:** *Write the name of the movie on your paper. Then draw a scene from the movie. Be sure the scene shows why the movie is so entertaining.* Allow time for students to share their scenes with the class.

◆ Explain that they can also evaluate the author's purpose when they read stories. Write the following on chart paper:

Movie Review

Think of a movie and write the title below. Then draw an entertaining scene from the movie.

Title of Movie: _____

Campfire Stories

Look at the blurb on the back of each book. Then draw a circle around the best answer to the question.

Time for stories!
Once upon a time,
a monster lived in
the woods . . .

In this book, the author probably wants to:

entertain readers by telling some scary stories

persuade readers to have a backyard campout

In this book, the author probably wants to:

inform readers how to start a campfire

entertain readers with a story about forest animals

Thank you for meeting
me at the campfire.
We must decide what
to do about Porcupine.

Draw a picture that might be in one of the books.

Guess!

Read the riddles. Then complete the sentence.

When is a girl like a bear?

When she is bear-foot!

What letter can buzz?

The letter B!

What color is loud?

Yell-ow!

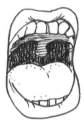

The author probably wants to _____.

Draw a picture about one of the riddles.

Catch the Moon

Read the story.

One day, the moon ran away.

"It's too dark!" the people cried.

Big Bob had to do something.

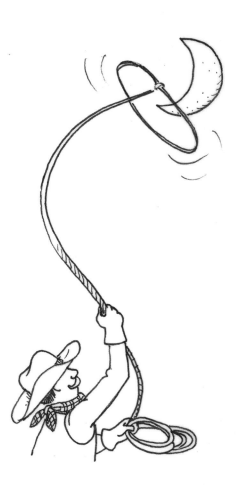

Out came Big Bob's lasso.

He swung it in the air.

He grabbed that moon.

He pulled it back.

He tied it tight.

"Now stay where you belong!" he said.

"Our hero!" the people said.

The author's purpose is  _____.

Draw a line under the clues in the story.

Assessment

Read the poem.

What a day, oh, what a day!

My cat and dog both ran away.

My dad is cross,

My mom is busy,

I have to play

with cousin Lizzy.

What a day, oh what a day!

Who made this day up, anyway?

Write the clues. Then write the author's purpose.

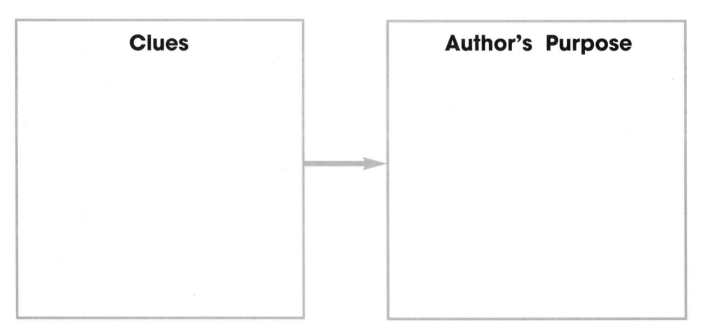

Clues	Author's Purpose

Overview Evaluating Author's Purpose in Nonfiction

Directions and Sample Answers for Activity Pages

Day 1	See "Provide a Real-World Example" below.
Day 2	Read and discuss the back-cover blurbs. Then help students circle the author's purpose for each one and draw a picture that might be in one of the books. (inform readers about things they can do at a library; persuade readers to keep reading newspapers)
Day 3	Read and discuss the directions and sign. Then help students circle the author's purpose for each one. (The author is informing readers how to make a sandwich. The author is persuading readers to come into the store.)
Day 4	Read and discuss the book review. Help students answer the first question and color the evidence blue. Then help them answer the second question and color the evidence red. (**1.** the book. **Evidence:** all but the first and last lines. **2:** read the book. **Evidence:** first line; last line.)
Day 5	Read the passage. Ask students to write evidence about the author's purpose on the graphic organizer. Then ask them to record the author's purpose. Afterward, meet individually with students to discuss their results. Use their responses to plan further instruction and review. (**Evidence:** Every sentence describes or tells a fact about a hurricane. **Author's purpose:** to inform readers about hurricanes.)

Provide a Real-World Example

◆ Hand out the Day 1 activity page.

◆ **Say:** *I just watched a television program. It showed kids getting all kinds of exercise, indoors and out. It told how important exercise is. It also gave reasons why kids should get more exercise. From these clues, I could tell that the writers wanted to persuade viewers to get more exercise.*

◆ Ask students to Think/Pair/Share other things they see on television that try to get people to do things. Then **say:** *Think of an advertisement you've seen on TV that tries to get you to buy something. Write what the ad is for. Then draw a picture of the ad. Allow time for students to share their ads.*

◆ Explain that students can also evaluate an author's purpose when they read. Write the following on chart paper:

Evaluating Author's Purpose in Nonfiction

Find evidence in the pictures.

Find evidence in the words.

Think like the author.

Think about how the author tries to persuade or inform.

Buy It!

Think of an ad you've seen on television. Tell what the ad is for. Then draw a scene from the ad below.

This ad is for _____.

Read All About It

Look at the blurb on the back of each book.
Then draw a circle around the author's purpose.

In this book, the author probably wants to:

inform readers about things they can do
at a library

entertain readers with funny stories
about libraries

In this book, the author probably wants to:

entertain readers with interesting
newspaper articles

persuade readers to keep reading
newspapers

**Draw a picture that might be in
one of the books.**

Healthy Foods

Read the directions.

1. Get two pieces of bread.

2. Put peanut butter on one piece.

3. Then slice the banana. Put the slices on top of the peanut butter.

4. Put the other piece of bread on top.

5. Cut the sandwich in half.

6. Share it with a friend!

What is the author's purpose? Draw a circle around the best answer.

The author is informing readers how to make a sandwich.

The author is persuading readers to eat a sandwich.

Read the sign.

Eat healthy food!

We have fresh vegetables and fruit.

Healthy foods are good for your body.

They taste good, too!

What is the author's purpose? Draw a circle around the best answer.

The author is informing readers about healthy food.

The author is persuading readers to come into the store.

   Unit 22 • Everyday Comprehension Intervention Activities Grade 2 • © 2010 Newmark Learning, LLC

Dear Pen Pal

Read the book review. Then answer the questions.

Dear Pen Pal is a great book.

It is about a girl and her friend.

The girls have never seen each other.

Instead, they write letters.

The girls tell about the places they live.

They tell about what they eat and play.

Give this book a try. You will like it!

1. The author wants to inform readers about _____.

    Color this evidence blue.

2. The author wants to persuade readers to _____.

    Color this evidence red.

Assessment

Read the passage.

A hurricane is a storm.

It has fast winds.

The winds whirl around in a circle.

Rain pours down.

A hurricane starts on the ocean.

It goes on and on for days.

Then it moves toward land.

The wind gets faster.

More rain falls.

The hurricane reaches land.

Finally, it slows down.

Write the evidence. Then write the author's purpose.

Evidence	Author's Purpose

Overview Analyzing Text Structure and Organization in Fiction

Directions and Sample Answers for Activity Pages

Day 1	See "Provide a Real-World Example" below.
Day 2	Read the sentences and discuss the pictures. Then help students draw a circle around the correct text structure for each set. (Sequence of Events; Compare and Contrast)
Day 3	Read the sentences and discuss the pictures. Then help students draw a line to the name of the correct text structure. (**1:** Problem and Solution. **2:** Compare and Contrast. **3:** Cause and Effect.)
Day 4	Read about Casey. Then help students follow the directions in each box. (Responses will vary.)
Day 5	Read the story together. Ask students to write clues on the graphic organizer. Then ask them to name the text structure. Afterward, meet individually with students to discuss their results. Use their responses to plan further instruction and review. (**Clues:** Leo forgot his homework. He tried to figure out what to do. Then Dad brought his homework. **Text structure:** Problem and Solution.)

Provide a Real-World Example

◆ Hand out the Day 1 activity page.

◆ **Say:** *I just had a postcard from a friend. She told me about a beach she visited. She told me what she saw. She told me what she heard. She told me how the sand felt beneath her toes. She even told me how the food at the snack stand smelled and tasted. From these clues, I could tell my friend was describing her trip to the beach.*

◆ Ask students to read the description of the backyard. Then ask them to draw a picture based on the description. Allow time for students to compare their drawings with their classmates' drawings.

◆ **Say:** *Description is one type of text structure we find when we read stories. We also find four other text structures.* Write the following on chart paper:

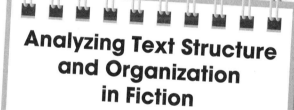

Analyzing Text Structure and Organization in Fiction

Look for:
- **words that describe**
- **words that compare and contrast**
- **words that tell about cause and effect**
- **words that tell about a sequence of events**
- **words that tell about a problem and a solution**

Favorite Backyard

Read the description. Then draw a picture based on what you've read.

Do you have a favorite backyard? I do!

Soft, green grass covers the ground.

A swing set is in one corner.

Yellow flowers grow by the fence.

Butterflies love how the flowers taste and smell!

Cool breezes swing the hammock between the trees.

Bird

Read the sentences. Look at each group of pictures. Think about the clues.
Then draw a circle around the correct text structure.

"Water, here I come!" said Bird.

Text Structure:

Description

Sequence of Events

Compare and Contrast

Cause and Effect

Problem and Solution

"Hmm . . . worms or seeds?" thought Bird.

Text Structure:

Description

Sequence of Events

Compare and Contrast

Cause and Effect

Problem and Solution

Best Friends

**Read the sentences. Look at the pictures. Think about the clues. Then draw a line
to the name of the text structure.**

1. "I lost my rocket ship," said Ari.

   "You can share mine!" said Ori.

2. "I'll carry the mitts," said Mae.

   "I'll carry the bats," said Asa.

3. "Why are you smiling?" asked Miley.

   "Because YOU'RE here!" said Grandpa.

Description

Sequence of Events

Compare and Contrast

Cause and Effect

Problem and Solution

Casey's Ice Cream

Read about Casey.

Casey has an ice cream cone. Yum!

Description: Write three words that describe ice cream.

Sequence of Events: Draw or write how to make an ice cream cone.

Compare and Contrast: Draw or write about two kinds of ice cream.

Cause and Effect: Draw or write what happens when the sun shines on an ice cream cone.

Problem and Solution: Casey dropped his cone. What should he do?

Assessment

Read the story.

"Oh no!" said Leo. "I forgot my homework!"

"What are you going to do?" asked Jill.

"I could hurry back home," said Leo.

"I could ask to use the phone.

I could bring it tomorrow."

Just then, Leo saw Dad.

"Here's your homework, Leo!" said Dad.

"I took it to work with me!"

Write clues from the story. Then name the text structure.

Clues	Text Structure

Overview Analyzing Text Structure and Organization in Nonfiction

Directions and Sample Answers for Activity Pages

Day 1	See "Provide a Real-World Example" below.
Day 2	Read the passage and discuss the pictures. Then help students draw a circle around the correct text structures. (Description; Compare and Contrast)
Day 3	Read and discuss the passages. Then help students write the name of the text structure on the line. (Cause and Effect; Problem and Solution)
Day 4	Read about bake sales. Then help students follow the directions in each box. (Responses will vary.)
Day 5	Read the ad together. Ask students to write evidence on the graphic organizer. Then ask them to name the text structure. Afterward, meet individually with students to discuss their results. Use their responses to plan further instruction and review. (**Evidence:** Each word and phrase tells something about the chairs. **Text structure:** Description.)

Provide a Real-World Example

◆ Hand out the Day 1 activity page.

◆ **Say:** *I just read a book about making greeting cards. First, it told how to fold the paper. Then it told where to write a message. Finally, it told how to decorate the card. From this evidence, I knew the text structure was a sequence of events. In a how-to text, we also call this text structure steps in a process.*

◆ Ask students to number the pictures on the page to show the correct order. Then ask them to read the passage and draw pictures to show the sequence of events. Allow time for students to share their drawings.

◆ **Say:** *Sequence of events is one type of text structure we find when we read. We also find four other text structures.* Write the following on chart paper:

Analyzing Text Structure and Organization in Nonfiction

Look for:
- **words that describe**
- **words that compare and contrast**
- **words that tell about cause and effect**
- **words that tell about a sequence of events**
- **words that tell about a problem and a solution**

1, 2, 3

Number the pictures below to show the correct order.

_____ _____ _____

Read the passage. Then draw pictures to show the sequence of events.

We have a pool in our yard.

First, we fill it with water.

Then we jump in.
We play for a long time.

Finally, we get out and dry off in the sun.

Puppets

Read the passage. Look at the pictures.

There are many kinds of puppets.

Some are made from socks.

Others are made from paper and paint.

Some are as big as a person.

Others fit on the tip of your finger.

But all puppets are colorful and fun.

**This passage uses two text structures. Think about the evidence.
Then draw a circle around the correct text structures.**

Text Structure:

Description

Sequence of Events

Compare and Contrast

Cause and Effect

Problem and Solution

Fun and Games

**Read the passages. Think about the evidence.
Then write the name of the text structure on the line.**

Word Bank		
Description	Compare and Contrast	Problem and Solution
Sequence of Events	Cause and Effect	

How do you decide what game to play?

Sometimes the weather helps you decide!

If the weather is nice, you can play games outside.

If the weather is bad, you can choose an indoor game.

_____

Rules help us play games.

But sometimes people must figure out their own rules.

Four friends come to your house.

You decide to play a board game.

The rules say only four people can play.

You make a rule.

You will watch this time!

_____

Bake Sales

Read about bake sales.

Many schools and clubs have bake sales.

People like to come to bake sales.

Bake sales are a good way to earn money.

Description: Think of something you would like to buy at a bake sale. Write three words to describe it.

Sequence of Events: A man buys a cookie that costs ten cents. The man gives you a quarter. Write what you would do next.

Compare and Contrast: Draw or write about two different places you could have a bake sale.

Cause and Effect: Draw or write what happens when someone reads a sign about a bake sale.

Problem and Solution: What would you do if rain started to fall during your bake sale?

Assessment

Read the ad.

Chairs for sale!

Old.

Need repairs.

Peeling paint.

Cracked wood.

A great deal!

Only $100 each!

Write evidence from the story. Then name the text structure.

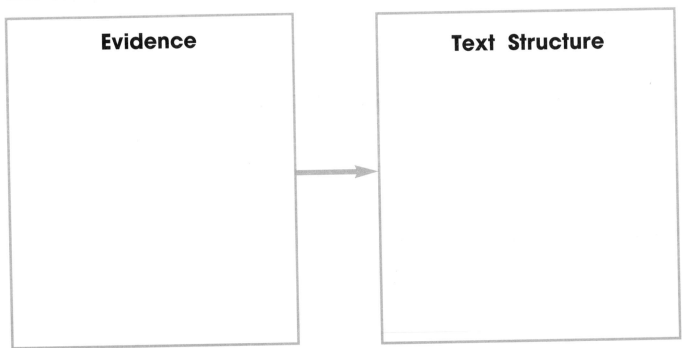

Evidence

Text Structure

Overview Using Text Features to Locate Information I

Directions and Sample Answers for Activity Pages

Day 1	See "Provide a Real-World Example" below.
Day 2	Read and discuss the front cover and title page. Then help students complete the sentences. (**1:** *Symbols of Our Country.* **2:** Penny Barry. **3:** both have the title, author, and a picture. **4:** they have different pictures. **5:** symbols in America, such as the flag, Liberty Bell, bald eagle, and Statue of Liberty. **6:** Responses will vary.)
Day 3	Read and discuss the table of contents. Then help students answer the questions. (**1:** page 2. **2:** page 12. **3:** Chapter 1. **4:** Chapter 2. **5:** Responses will vary. **6:** Introduction and/or Conclusion.)
Day 4	Discuss the pictures and captions. Help students answer the questions under each caption. Then ask them to write a new caption for one of the pictures. (***Tornado!:*** yes, no. ***Alexander Graham Bell:*** yes, no. ***Pollution:*** yes, yes. **Student's caption:** Responses will vary.)
Day 5	Provide each student with a nonfiction book that includes a front cover, title page, table of contents, chapter headings, and captions. Ask students to use the book to complete the chart. Afterward, meet individually with students to discuss their results. Use their responses to plan further instruction and review. (Responses will vary.)

Provide a Real-World Example

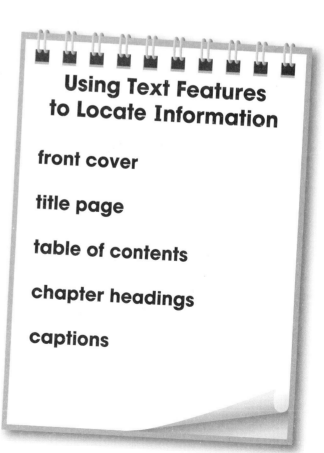

- ◆ Select a nonfiction book with a front cover, title page, table of contents, chapter headings, and captions. Provide each student with a nonfiction book.
- ◆ Hand out the Day 1 activity page.
- ◆ **Say:** *Nonfiction books have certain text features. We use these text features to locate, or find, information in the book.*
- ◆ Hold up your book. **Say:** *First, I will look at the front cover. The front cover shows the title and author of the book.* Point to the title and author's name as you read them aloud.
- ◆ **Say:** *Look at your book. Does your book have a front cover? Read the title and author's name to a partner. Then put a check mark in the front cover box on your chart.*
- ◆ Repeat the process for the remaining text features, first pointing one out in your book and then asking students to see if it is included in their books. Discuss their findings.
- ◆ **Say:** *This week we will learn more about these text features.* Write the following on chart paper:

Using Text Features to Locate Information

front cover

title page

table of contents

chapter headings

captions

My Book

Choose a nonfiction book. Does your book have the following text features? Put a check mark next to features your book has.

front cover	
title page	
table of contents	
chapter headings	
captions	

Front Cover and Title Page

Look at the front cover and title page. Then complete the sentences.

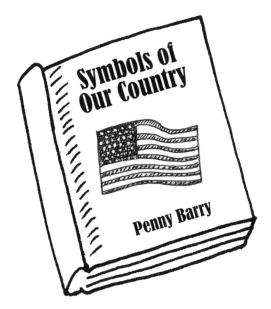

Front Cover

Title Page

1. The title of the book is _____.

2. The author is _____.

3. The front cover and title page are alike because

_____.

4. The front cover and title page are different because

_____.

5. The book will probably be about

_____.

6. Another good title for this book might be

_____.

Table of Contents and Chapter Headings

Look at the table of contents. Read the chapter headings. Then answer the questions.

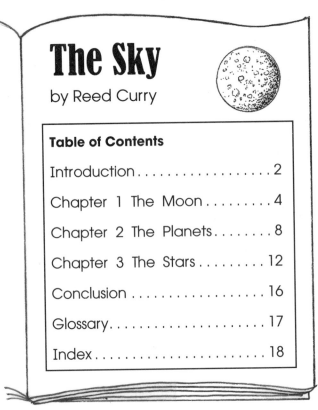

The Sky
by Reed Curry

Table of Contents

1. On what page will you begin reading the book? _____

2. What page would you go to if you want to learn about stars? _____

3. Which chapter might tell about the phases of the moon? _____

4. Which chapter might have a diagram showing the locations of the planets? _____

5. What is one thing you might read about in Chapter 2?

_____

6. Where would you find information about the whole book? _____

   Unit 25 • Everyday Comprehension Intervention Activities Grade 2 • © 2010 Newmark Learning, LLC

Captions

A caption gives information about a picture. A caption can also ask a question.
Read each caption. Then mark YES or NO.

Title of Book: *Tornado!*

Tornadoes are shaped like funnels.

Does this caption tell about the picture?   Yes   No

Does this caption ask a question?   Yes   No

Title of Book: *Alexander Graham Bell*

Bell's most famous invention is the telephone.

Does this caption tell about the picture?   Yes   No

Does this caption ask a question?   Yes   No

Title of Book: *Pollution*

How can you help prevent water pollution?

Does this caption tell about the picture?   Yes   No

Does this caption ask a question?   Yes   No

Choose one of the pictures. Write a new caption.

_____.

Assessment

Use your book to complete the chart.

	Where did I find it in the book?	What is one thing I can learn from this text feature?
front cover		
title page		
table of contents		
chapter headings		
captions		

Overview Using Text Features to Locate Information II

Directions and Sample Answers for Activity Pages

Day 1	See "Provide a Real-World Example" below.
Day 2	Read the sidebars together. Then help students rate the sidebars and explain their ratings. (Responses will vary.)
Day 3	Read and discuss the passage and glossary. Then help students answer the questions. (**1:** glossary. **2:** what is left of animals or plants that lived long ago. **3:** a reptile that lived millions of years ago. **4.** alphabetical (or ABC). **5:** fossils. **6:** Responses will vary.)
Day 4	Read and discuss the index. Then help students answer the questions. (**1:** page 8. **2:** pages 4–5. **3:** hunting and Weddell seals. **4:** in alphabetical (or ABC) order. **5:** seals. **6:** Responses will vary.)
Day 5	Provide each student with a nonfiction book that includes a sidebar, boldfaced words, a glossary, and an index. Ask students to use the book to complete the chart. Afterward, meet individually with students to discuss their results. Use their responses to plan further instruction and review. (Responses will vary.)

Provide a Real-World Example

◆ Select a nonfiction book with sidebars, boldfaced words, a glossary, and an index. Provide each student with a nonfiction book.

◆ Hand out the Day 1 activity page. Review the text features from the previous unit. Invite students to mark their charts to show which ones are included in their books.

◆ **Say:** *Nonfiction books have other text features, too. One text feature is a sidebar. A sidebar tells more about the information in a book.* Point out several sidebars in your book and read them aloud.

◆ **Say:** *Look at your book. Does your book have sidebars? Choose one to show your partner. Then put a check mark in the sidebars box on your chart.*

◆ Repeat the process for the remaining text features, first pointing one out in your book and then asking students to see if it is included in their books. Discuss their findings.

◆ **Say:** *Let's add these new text features to our chart.* Display the chart created in the previous unit and add the remaining text features to the list.

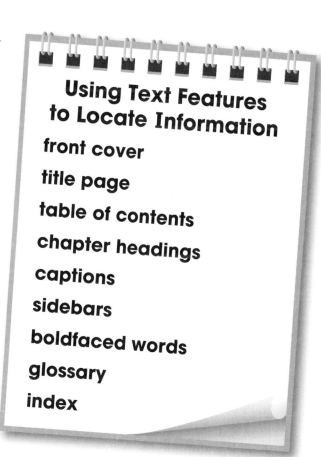

Using Text Features to Locate Information
front cover
title page
table of contents
chapter headings
captions
sidebars
boldfaced words
glossary
index

Front to Back

Choose a nonfiction book.

front cover	
title page	
table of contents	
chapter headings	
captions	
sidebars	
boldfaced words	
glossary	
index	

Sidebars

A sidebar tells more information about a person, animal, place, object, or event. These sidebars are from a book called *All About Animals*. Rate each sidebar. Then explain your rating.

Busy Beavers

Beavers create ponds. These ponds are good for the environment. The ponds become homes for other animals. Ducks, geese, and otters live in beaver ponds.

This sidebar is

❑ good

❑ fair

❑ poor.

I chose this rating because

_____

_____ .

When Is a Dog Not a Dog?

Prairie dogs are not really dogs at all. They are not even related to dogs. They are rodents, like mice and squirrels. Prairie dogs got their name from the noise they make. They sound like barking dogs!

This sidebar is

❑ good

❑ fair

❑ poor.

I chose this rating because

_____

_____ .

Boldfaced Words and Glossary

Read the passage. Look at the boldfaced words. Find the words in the glossary. Then complete the sentences.

Glossary

dinosaur: a reptile that lived millions of years ago

fossils: what is left of animals or plants that lived long ago

organisms: living plants or animals

paleontologist: a scientist who studies fossils

tar pit: an area where animals became trapped in a sticky substance long ago

Fossils are what is left of animals or plants that lived long ago. You can look at bone fossils from a **dinosaur**. These bones were left behind when the dinosaur died. Over time, the bones turned into rock.

1. The boldfaced words are also in the _____.

2. The first boldfaced word means _____.

3. The second boldfaced word means _____.

4. The words in the glossary are in _____ order.

5. This book is probably about _____.

6. A good title for this book might be _____.

Index

**Look at the index.
Then answer the questions.**

Index

Antarctica, 2–3

flippers, 8

fur, 7

hunting, 11–13

ice, 3, 6–7

seals, 4–6

seal pups, 4–5

Weddell seals, 4–11, 13

1. On which page will you find information about flippers? _____

2. What pages would you go to if you wanted to read about seal pups? _____

3. What is page 13 about? _____

4. How are the words in the index arranged? _____

5. What is this book probably about? _____

6. What might be a good title for this book? _____

Assessment

Use your book to complete the chart.

	Where did I find it in the book?	What is one thing I can learn from this text feature?
sidebar		
boldfaced words		
glossary		
index		

Overview Using Graphic Features to Interpret Information I

Directions and Sample Answers for Activity Pages

Day 1	See "Provide a Real-World Example" below.
Day 2	Discuss each illustration and why the author might have used it instead of a photograph. Then help students color in the circle in front of the best reason. (**Plant:** It shows parts we could not see in a photograph. **Abraham Lincoln:** It is from long ago when people didn't have cameras. **Ship:** It shows something people imagined.)
Day 3	Discuss each labeled diagram. Then help students circle the facts they learn. (**Cube:** This is a cube. A cube has squares. A cube has corners. A face is a square on a cube. **Sun and planets:** The sun is in the middle. Mercury is closest to the sun. Mars has more moons than Earth has. The planets move around the sun.)
Day 4	Discuss the maps and their special features. Then help students complete the sentences. (**First map:** France, Paris, the Seine River/Loire River/Rhône River. **Second map:** Pirate Cove, east, Sun-Baked Desert.)
Day 5	Read the name of each graphic feature. Then ask students to use the graphic features to complete the chart. Afterward, meet individually with students to discuss their results. Use their responses to plan further instruction and review. (Responses will vary.)

Provide a Real-World Example

◆ Select a nonfiction book with photographs and inset photos. Provide each student with a nonfiction book.

◆ **Say:** *Nonfiction texts have graphic features. Readers must know how to interpret, or figure out, the information on a graphic feature. One important graphic feature is a photograph. We can learn a lot from a photograph!*

◆ Share some photographs from your book and what readers can learn from them. Point out any inset photos as well, noting how they provide additional details about the larger photograph. Then invite students to look through their own books and find a photograph to share with the group.

◆ Hand out the Day 1 activity page and discuss the photograph. Ask students to write words and phrases that tell what they learn from the photograph on the lines around it.

◆ **Say:** *This week we will learn about some other graphic features, too.* Write the following on chart paper:

Using Graphic Features to Interpret Information

photographs and inset photos

illustrations

labeled diagrams

maps

Photo Search

Look at the photograph of the book cover. Write what you learn from looking at the book cover.

Illustrations

Some nonfiction texts have illustrations. Look at each illustration. Think about why the author used an illustration instead of a photograph. Then color in the circle in front of the best reason.

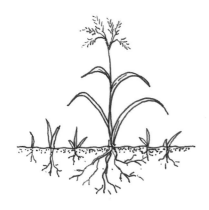

○ It is from long ago when people didn't have cameras.

○ It shows parts we could not see in a photograph.

○ It shows something people imagined.

○ It is from long ago when people didn't have cameras.

○ It shows parts we could not see in a photograph.

○ It shows something people imagined.

○ It is from long ago when people didn't have cameras.

○ It shows parts we could not see in a photograph.

○ It shows something people imagined.

Labeled Diagrams

Look at each labeled diagram. Draw a circle around the facts you learn from the diagram.

This is a square.

This is a cube.

A cube has squares.

A cube has corners.

A face is a corner on a cube.

A face is a square on a cube.

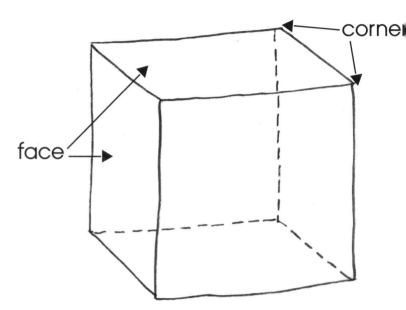

Earth is in the middle.

The sun is in the middle.

Mercury is closest to the sun.

Mars is closest to the sun.

Mars has more moons than Earth does.

The planets move around the sun.

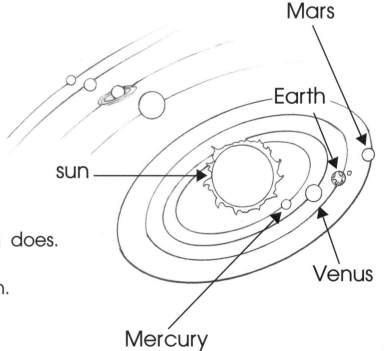

Unit 27 • Everyday Comprehension Intervention Activities Grade 2 • © 2010 Newmark Learning, LLC

Maps

Look at each map. Then complete the sentences.

This is a map of a country.

The country is _____.

The star shows the capital city of the country.

The capital city is _____.

The thin lines show rivers in the country.

One river is _____.

This is a map of an island.

Ships can land at

_____.

The arrows show which way is north, east, south, and west.

The Mysterious Mountains are _____ of Good Luck Lake.

You can use the numbers and letters to name the squares.

You find

_____ in

square 2E.

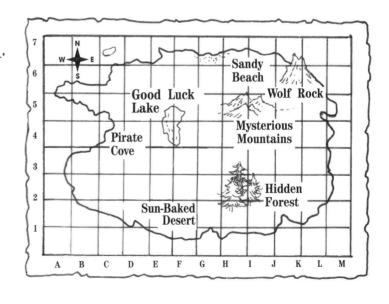

Assessment

Look at each graphic feature. Then complete the chart.

		What is one thing I can learn from this graphic feature?
photograph		
illustration		
labeled diagram		
map		

Overview Using Graphic Features to Interpret Information II

Directions and Sample Answers for Activity Pages

Day 1	See "Provide a Real-World Example" below.
Day 2	Read and discuss each table and its special features. Then help students answer the questions. (**Table A: 1.** orange juice and skim milk. **2.** 2 grams. **3.** 50 calories. **4.** scrambled eggs. **5.** skim milk. **Table B: 1.** 3 teaspoons. **2.** 8 tablespoons. **3.** 1 cup. **4.** a tablespoon. **5.** 3/4 cup.)
Day 3	Read and discuss the weather chart. Then help students complete the sentences. (**1.** Sunday. **2.** Thursday. **3.** Tuesday. **4.** Wednesday and Thursday. **5.** Friday and Saturday.) Then ask students to fill in the "Things to Do" chart.
Day 4	Read and discuss the pie graph and bar graph. Then help students circle the facts they learn. (**Pie graph:** Most beach trash is plastic. People leave about the same amount of paper and metal on beaches. Some people leave wood or rubber items on beaches. **Bar graph:** Mexico City . . . had more cars in 2005 than in 1995; had more than 3 million cars in 2005; had fewer than 3 million cars in 1995.)
Day 5	Read the name of each graphic feature. Then ask students to use the graphic features to complete the chart. Afterward, meet individually with students to discuss their results. Use their responses to plan further instruction and review. (Responses will vary.)

Provide a Real-World Example

◆ Hand out the Day 1 activity page.

◆ **Say:** *We have learned that nonfiction texts have graphic features. Another graphic feature is a time line. A time line shows things that have happened and when they happened.*

◆ Ask students to look at the time line on the page. **Say:** *This time line shows different types of buildings people in the United States have helped build. The first year on the time line is 1780. People built a Puritan house in 1780. Draw a line from the year 1780 on the time line to the picture of the Puritan house.*

◆ Repeat the process with the other dates and buildings (1870—log cabin; 1940—skyscraper; 1960—ranch-style house; 2001—International Space Station). Then discuss how the time line shows the history of building.

◆ **Say:** *This week we will learn about some other graphic features, too. I will add the new graphic features to our chart.* Display the chart created in the previous unit and add the remaining graphic features to the list.

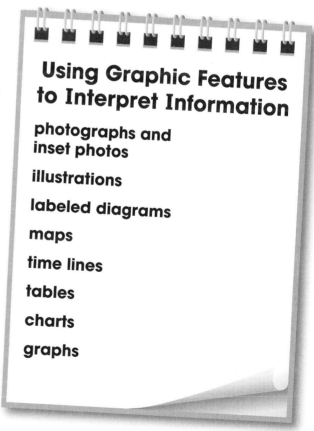

Using Graphic Features to Interpret Information

photographs and inset photos

illustrations

labeled diagrams

maps

time lines

tables

charts

graphs

Building Time Line

Draw a line from the year to the
matching building.

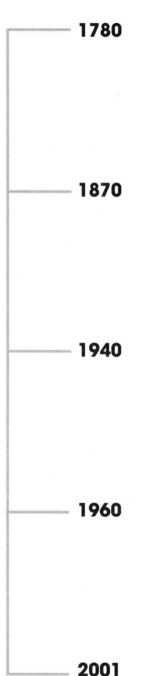

1780

1870

1940

1960

2001

skyscraper

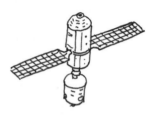

**International
Space Station**

Puritan house

ranch-style house

log cabin

Food Tables

Read each table. Then answer the questions.

TABLE A			
	Amount	Fat (g)	Calories
Orange juice	1 cup	0	110
Scrambled eggs	2	14	200
Margarine, low-calorie	1 tbsp.	5	50
Milk, skim	1 cup	0	90
Toast	2 slices	2	130

TABLE A

1. Which items have no fat grams? _____

2. How many fat grams are in 2 slices of toast? _____

3. How many calories are in 1 tablespoon of low-calorie margarine? ___

4. Which food has the most fat grams and calories? _____

5. Which food has 90 calories in 1 cup? _____

TABLE B

1. How many teaspoons are in 1 tablespoon? _____

2. How many tablespoons are in 1/2 cup? _____

3. How many cups are equal to 16 tablespoons? _____

4. Which is more—a teaspoon or a tablespoon? _____

5. Which is more—3/4 cup or 4 tablespoons? _____

TABLE B		
3 teaspoons	=	1 tablespoon
4 tablespoons	=	¼ cup
8 tablespoons	=	½ cup
12 tablespoons	=	¾ cup
16 tablespoons	=	1 cup

Charts

A chart shows information that can be different from day to day. Look at the weather chart. Then complete the sentences.

Sunday	Monday	Tuesday	Wednesday	Thursday	Friday	Saturday
Mostly cloudy	Rain	Thunderstorms	Sunny	Sunny	Partly cloudy	Rain
High 51° Low 38°	High 49° Low 39°	High 50° Low 42°	High 56° Low 47°	High 57° Low 45°	High 55° Low 41°	High 54° Low 41°

1. The coldest day was _____.

2. The warmest day was _____.

3. _____ had thunderstorms.

4. _____ and _____ were sunny.

5. _____ and _____ had the same low temperature.

A chart shows information that can be different from person to person. Fill in this chart. Then share your chart with a classmate.

Things to Do	alone	with friends
ride a bike		
read a book		
play ball		
watch TV		
eat ice cream		
go to the movies		
visit my grandmother		

Graphs

A graph is another way to show information. Look at the pie graph and bar graph. Draw a circle around the facts you learn from each graph.

Most beach trash is plastic.

The smallest amount of beach trash is glass.

People leave about the same amount of paper and metal on beaches.

Some people leave wood or rubber items on beaches.

People should leave more plastic on beaches.

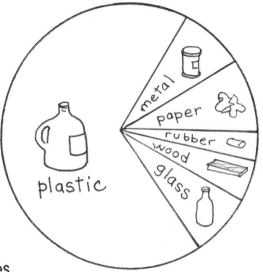

Mexico City . . .

has over 5 million cars.

had more cars in 2005 than in 1995.

had fewer cars in 2005 than in 1995.

had more than 3 million cars in 2005.

had fewer than 3 million cars in 1995.

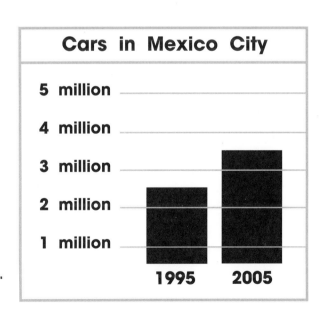

Assessment

Look at each graphic feature. Then complete the chart.

		What is one thing I can learn from this graphic feature?
time line	▼ ▼ ▼ Early 1800s 1885 1903 bicycle first car airplane	
table	**Multiply** 1 2 3 2 4 6 3 6 9	
chart	**Class Jobs** **Lead Line** Joe **Run Errands** Lin **Feed Pet** Max	
graph	**The Air We Breathe** oxygen nitrogen	

Notes

Notes

Everyday Comprehension Intervention Activities Grade 2 • ©2010 Newmark Learning, LLC